SPIRIT OF

Cooking from Ranch House and Range

THE WEST

SPIRIT OF

Cooking from Ranch House and Range

THE WEST

BEVERLY COX *and* MARTIN JACOBS

ARTISAN *New York*

EDITOR: Ann ffolliott

PRODUCTION DIRECTOR: Hope Koturo

Published in 1996 by Artisan,
a division of
Workman Publishing Company, Inc.
708 Broadway
New York, NY 10003-9555

LIBRARY OF CONGRESS
CATALOGING-IN-PUBLICATION DATA

Cox, Beverly, 1945 –
Spirit of the West :
cooking from ranch house and range /
by Beverly Cox and Martin Jacobs.
Includes bibliographic references and index.
ISBN 1-885183-21-6
1. Cookery, American—Western style.
1. Jacobs, Martin.
II. Title.
TX715.2.W47C68   1996
96-21063
641.5978--dc20   CIP

Printed in Italy
10 9 8 7 6 5 4 3 2 1
First Printing

DEDICATION

THIS BOOK IS DEDICATED TO MY GRANDMOTHER MAY KETCHAM COX, WHO WAS BORN ON A RANCH NEAR THE OUTSKIRTS OF CHEYENNE IN 1881, WHEN WYOMING WAS STILL A TERRITORY. SHE HAD "SPUNK," A QUALITY MUCH ADMIRED IN THE WEST. GRANDMA COX WAS A FRONTIER WOMAN WHO RODE HORSES, PRESIDED OVER TEA PARTIES, AND SHOT RATTLESNAKES WITH EQUAL APLOMB. SHE WAS A LIVELY COMPANION FOR A SMALL GIRL AND IS OFTEN IN MY THOUGHTS TODAY.

— Beverly Cox

CONTENTS

THE BEEPING ALARM of my wristwatch woke me at a quarter to four in the morning. My wife Carrie and I crawled out of a warm bed into a very cold room. It was -18° Fahrenheit outside—cold enough to freeze the ears off a brass monkey! We had spent the night at Brian Ward's spacious log house in Colorado's south-central San Luis Valley. The reason for rising so early was a buffalo drive. Five hundred cows (female buffalo) were waiting for us to move them thirty-four miles across the valley to a new pasture. It would take two days.

We pulled on blue jeans and warm, heavy, Pendleton shirts, stuffed wool-stockinged feet into cold boots, and—after a pass with razor and comb for me—descended the stairs to the kitchen below. Diane, Brian's wife, was already up, dressed, and making coffee. How good it smelled! Soon the kitchen was crowded with arriving cowboys, about a dozen of them, wrapped up like grizzly bears in heavy coats. No dudes, these. With Brian, they would drive the herd to the Zapata Ranch across the valley.

Talk about frying pans! Huge, wide ones, which we'd later use on the trail, served this morning as stove griddles for fried hen fruit, ham, and sourdough flapjacks. The men needed a sturdy breakfast, for it wasn't easy going out there in the snow. Buffalo don't take too kindly to herd-moving in this kind of weather.

Brian and Diane's young kids had jobs, too. The boy, perhaps six, stood on the back of a tractor-pulled wagon filled with bales of hay. As his dad drove slowly in front of the herd, the youngster pushed feed off the back. The buffaloes began to follow, rising and breaking into a trot. It was a responsible job, and the boy knew he had better hold onto the wagon with one hand, lest he fall in the path of several hundred hungry cows.

Ranch children learn two things early: (1) Always close the gate. (2) Keep your word. "Closing the gate" means being responsible for your own actions. Forgetting and carelessly leaving a gate open can cost your family its horses, cattle, and livelihood. And in the real West, they don't put much stock in Dun & Bradstreet or Metro Credit Reports. They simply ask around: "Is his word good?" If people they respect say yes, then they trust the person. So it's drummed into the kids very early that one's word is to be protected and honored.

At five A.M., everyone mounted up, and the drive began. "Move 'em out!" The dozen cowboys—plus two cowgirls, including Carrie—set out for Zapata Ranch, with five hundred buffalo cows in front of them. No *mooing* here; Buffalo chuff or grunt. But the main difference

OPPOSITE: *Roundup Fried Potatoes and Eggs. See recipe, page 66.*

between moving beef cattle and buffalo is that buffalo are brainier. They're looking for something perverse to do, like take off at a right angle from the route they're supposed to follow.

My job was to go down the line a few miles and set up a cooking camp by the road where the buffalo drive would pass. Randy, superintendent of the Zapata Ranch, had his pickup truck loaded with me and the goods: firewood, starter, grates, huge pans, six two-pound packages of bacon, sliced onions, sliced cooked potatoes (4 gallons!), shoe peg corn kernels, half-gallon tubs of chopped green chilies, salt and pepper, utensils, paper plates, cups, coffeepots, and ground coffee. Knowing the territory and proposed route, Randy drove us about twenty miles from Brian's house. He picked a site beside the road and we built a big fire.

Then the word came that the buffaloes had decided they didn't like Brian's southbound route, and they preferred to run east toward the mountains. So we killed the fire and followed the cowboys and -girls as they chased the herd for six miles or more. After a half hour of fast riding across the valley, the cowboys turned the leaders, getting them headed southward again onto a dirt road. Randy and I quickly built another fire four miles south of our first one. When the cowboys arrived with the herd, about an hour later, two giant, sizzling frying pans were loaded with crisp fried bacon, potatoes, onions, corn and spicy green chile. Big spatulas allowed us to keep turning the mixture as it browned deliciously over a very hot fire. The scent of bacon and onions made the mouth water! In addition, a large grill held several dozen thick buffalo burgers, just ready as the cowboys approached. Without dismounting, the riders feasted on platefuls of "Sam's Buffalo-Drive Taters" and big juicy burgers, swilled down with tin cups of freshly cooked camp coffee.

It took nine hours in the saddle the first day, and five more on the second. Everyone arrived safely, if a bit tired and cold, and Randy and I shared some welcome peppermint schnapps and hot coffee in his truck.

This buffalo drive was a new experience for me. For although I've lived nearly half a century in the West, I'm an urban product—born and raised in Denver—and until now contemporary cowboy life hadn't touched mine. To me cowboys were the "fellers" at dude ranches who took care of the horses. It's only in recent years that I've discovered there are ranches within a 45-minute drive of Denver, in virtually any direction. Ranch life thrives! Stories in the press about the demise of the ranchers and cowboys are inaccurate. Times change, but ranching is strong in spite of natural, economic, and political storms. Cattle and buffalo ranches abound in the West, but you don't see 'em unless you look. And if you don't believe that there's money to be made, mosey around the National Western Stock Show at Denver each January. It will amaze you.

That's why this book by Beverly Cox and Martin Jacobs is such a treasure. Raised in a Wyoming family with a long heritage of cattle ranching in both Wyoming and Colorado, Beverly has pulled together stories and recipes from the West's great family ranches, including her own. She takes us on a tour, beginning with the *vaquero* traditions of Mexican ranchers, and follows the history of Western cattle ranching from before the Civil War to today. She writes about tough times and periods of near starvation. But ranch cooking isn't all just basic beans, bacon, and corn pones. Today, ranches serve a wide variety of meats of different kinds and cuts, plus fruits and vegetables, fresh and dried. The recipes are here.

Ms. Cox traveled deep into Mexico's northern mountains, miles from main roads, to learn authentic recipes of present-day Mexican *vaqueros*. Don't be surprised to find a lot of canned goods in these recipes. This tradition goes way back in time to the beginnings of the nineteenth century, when canned products first became available. Canned tomatoes were the cowman's thirst quencher.

Perhaps the greatest delights found in this book are the recipes from Cox's wide acquaintance with ranch families. From 91-year-old Martha Fehlman in Powell, Wyoming, comes a dandy recipe for sour-milk pancakes. And if you're baking, it'd be hard to choose between the author's grandmother May Ketcham Cox's recipe for quick baking powder biscuits or the butterscotch rolls of the Ferguson family, fifth-generation Wyoming ranchers.

Don't think that this is only a cowboy cookbook. Out on the range, traveling from place to place, there weren't opportunities for the development of an extensive cuisine. But back at the ranch house was another matter. Edna Jones of Garden City, Kansas, for example, served up to the cowboys at her ranch a wonderful meal of "beef short ribs and pinto beans cooked together, with a side of cool pink applesauce, hot cornbread slathered with butter and honey, and tall glasses of iced tea."

Along with the recipes, *Spirit of the West* includes thumbnail biographies of many ranchers. Sample the Dakota Golden Pheasant Fricassee, which comes from the Huls ranch in Salem, South Dakota. Your stomach will rumble when you read about the Montana Pitchfork Fondue. Imagine that you and your friends are wielding pitchforks full of T-bone steaks, frying them in a huge cauldron of hot oil. Or consider the Grover, Colorado, Wiggin Ranch's Milk Can Suppers, in which eight- or ten-gallon milk cans are used for cooking up a huge stew of potatoes, carrots, corn, and sausages. What fun! The author has collected the fascinating and the unusual, with recipes to tease even the most sophisticated gourmand. Please now, dig in and savor the heritage of wonderful cowboy and ranch table delights!

—SAM'L P. ARNOLD
June 4, 1996

THE VAQUERO
TRADITION

IN NORTHERN MEXICO, NEW MEXICO,
ARIZONA, AND CALIFORNIA

*T*HE COWBOY is truly an American original, a hero to people around the world. He represents strength, individuality, and freedom from the restraints of modern urban life. But where does his story begin?

Without Christopher Columbus, the American cowboy might not exist. Columbus brought the first cattle to the new world in 1494 on his second voyage. Early in the sixteenth century, after Cortés conquered what is now Mexico, Spaniards brought cattle from the West Indies to New Spain. There the animals multiplied rapidly, but the Spaniards soon tired of caring for them. So the Spanish padres taught their new converts—Indians, African slaves, and other non-Spaniards—to ride horses and watch the cattle. Gradually the *vaquero*—the Mexican cowboy—was born. When the native Indians complained about Spanish cattle trampling their crops and the Spaniards complained about their cattle being rustled, the Spanish crown established an association of stock-raisers called the *Mesta*, which ordered cattle-raisers to brand their cattle, register their brands, and keep track of their strays.

As the Spanish frontier pushed northward from near Mexico City, cattle ranching moved with it, and the rugged country of Chihuahua, Coahuila, Nuevo Leon, and Durango in what is now northern Mexico became the traditional home of the Mexican *vaquero*. During the same period, the Spaniards modified their traditional tools and techniques to meet the *vaqueros'* needs. The saddle horn of the old Spanish saddles was enlarged so the *vaquero* could tie his *lazo* (lasso) to it when roping cattle. Once an animal was caught, the *vaquero* would quickly wrap his end of the *lazo* around the saddle horn. This technique was called *da la vuelta*, meaning "to turn around." Decades later cowboys north of the Rio Grande corrupted the Spanish phrase to "dally."

Many other tools and techniques used by modern cowboys can be traced to the *vaquero*, including the hackamore—derived from the Spanish word *jaquima*, meaning halter. Even the word *rodeo* comes from the Spanish *rodear*, meaning "to go around" or "to surround or encircle." First used to describe a cattle roundup, *rodeo* today means an exhibition of skills by cowboys.

The earliest *vaqueros* were working-class people, and they ate the modest foods of the native peoples of Mexico. Their daily fare consisted largely of corn tortillas and posole (hominy) combined with beans and chilies. This sounds like a sparse diet, but it is quite nutritious. Somehow, the pre-Columbian peoples of the Americas had discovered that hominy (corn treated with an alkaline substance such as lime) when combined with beans, was more nutritious than untreated corn and beans. Modern nutritionists would discover that these two foods, eaten in combination, form a complete protein. By eating hominy and beans, supplemented by other vitamin-rich native foods such as chilies, tomatoes, and peanuts, the early *vaqueros* ate better and probably lived longer than their European counterparts.

When the Spaniards first arrived in New Spain, turkeys were the only domesticated fowl, and dishes containing turkey were common among the wealthy inhabitants. But with the introduction of Spanish cattle, those who could afford it turned to beef, and turkey was more widely eaten by the poorer natives, including the *vaqueros*.

As the cattle hacienda system developed during the seventeenth century in what is now northern Mexico, *vaqueros* were sent to tend large herds far from their ranch headquarters. They slept under the stars or in a crude lean-toes and learned to live off the land. They would build their fire and cook their meals, which usually consisted of *atole* (corn meal porridge), dried *frijoles* (beans), *tortillas*, and beef or wild game—deer, wild boar (*javelina*), dove, turkey, rabbit, roadrunner (*paisano*), goat, fish, or quail—and pieces of nopal cactus. Their meat dishes were usually cooked in a highly seasoned ancho- or jalapeño-chile–flavored sauce. Occasionally they would enjoy a dish of prickly pear cactus cooked with wild birds eggs.

Like *frijoles*, *tortillas* were a mainstay of the *vaquero's* diet. Should a *vaquero* have no corn with which to make *tortillas*, he would look for the sweet beans of mesquite, with which he could make *mesquitemal*, a bread substitute.

The fruits of the *coyoniste* cactus and the *tunas* of prickly pear cactus could be eaten raw. If cooked, they were eaten like candy. A drink called *colonche* could also be made from the prickly pear. In addition to water, *vaqueros* occasionally drank *pulque*, a thick, milky-looking liquid concocted from *aguamiel*, the sap taken from the center of the maguey plant as it was about to bloom. The sap was permitted to ferment in a goat-, pig-, or sheepskin bag. In time, the popular drinks *mescal* and *tequila* were made from the same plant, using different processes.

As Spanish cattle-raising moved into California, Arizona, New Mexico, and Texas during the late seventeenth and early eighteenth centuries, it was only natural that the cuisine of the *vaquero* spread into these areas, modified depending upon the availability of wild game, corn, and chilies. Beef, however, was usually plentiful. As life became more civilized, the influence of the *vaquero* cuisine became evident in the everyday cooking of northern Mexico, Texas, New Mexico, Arizona, and California, and it became a mainstay of cuisine of south and west Texas. In Arizona, *vaquero* cuisine evolved into new and original forms, while in California, its Spanish elements survived. In New Mexico, it was absorbed by the Indians in their food preparation and became part of the cuisine unique to northern New Mexico.

Today the influence of the early *vaquero* survives in the saddles used by many American cowboys, in their lariats, in the techniques they use to handle cattle, and in many words sprinkled through their daily speech. But it is perhaps most evident in the cuisine of the Southwest.

—DAVID DARY

Beef and Pork Tamales

In the 1950s Señora Maria Louisa Salcido, a renowned cook from an old ranching family near Benson, Arizona, taught her friend Florence Gillespie to make tamales. Florence has been making great tamales ever since and has shared the recipe with us. Señora Salcido still lives on the beautiful mountain ranch where her family homesteaded in 1902. Her daughters are currently at work on a cookbook featuring the old recipes of the Salcido family.

To enhance the flavor of the tamale filling, cook the meat and prepare the sauce the day before you make tamales. If desired, you can use half lard and half vegetable shortening in the chile sauce, or substitute vegetable shortening for the lard. Traditionally, lard is used because it gives the best texture and flavor to the chile. For more information on lard, see the appendix.

The masa is made from a special ground white cornmeal labeled *Masa de Harina de Maiz*. You can buy it at many supermarkets. The following recipe makes enough masa for about one-fifth of the tamale meat filling. Don't make masa in larger batches because it may dry out before you use it. You can make extra batches of masa as you need it. Canned beef broth can be added to the masa mixture if you need additional liquid as you go along. For the best flavor, use the fat from the meat broth in the masa dough and mix it with enough lard or shortening to make the necessary full cup.

TAMALE MEAT FILLING

1 beef chuck roast (4 to 5 pounds)

1 pork shoulder roast (4 to 5 pounds)

1 onion, peeled (optional)

1 carrot (optional)

1 teaspoon salt

½ teaspoon ground black pepper

RED CHILE SAUCE

1 cup freshly ground red chile powder (hot, medium-hot, or mild)

1 cup lard

1¼ cups all-purpose flour

1 tablespoon salt

CORN HUSK WRAPPERS

3 (8-ounce) bags of prepared corn shucks

TAMALE MASA

5 to 5½ cups meat broth (reserved from the meat filling)

1 cup lard (reserved from the meat filling) or a mixture of lard and vegetable shortening

6 cups masa harina

3 tablespoons baking powder

2 teaspoons salt

To make the meat filling, place the beef and pork in a large stewpot with a lid. Add water to cover and the onion, carrot, salt, and pepper. Cover and cook over medium-high heat until tender, about 2 hours.

If the broth cooks down, add additional water. (The meat can be cut into smaller pieces for faster cooking.) Cover and refrigerate the meat in the broth overnight.

To make the chile sauce, mix the chile powder and 1 cup of water to make a paste, stirring until all the lumps are gone. Add 1 more cup of water, stir until smooth and set aside. In a large frying pan, melt the lard over medium-high heat. Add the flour all at once and stir constantly until lightly browned. Continue to stir because the mixture can quickly burn if left untended. Add the salt and 6 cups of water and stir well. Add the chile mixture and stir until smooth. Cook over low heat for about 30 minutes, being careful to stir often. Chile can scorch very quickly. If the mixture seems too thick, add a little water to thin it. The consistency should be similar to that of a thick gravy. Transfer to a bowl and allow to cool slightly, then cover and refrigerate overnight to blend the flavors.

The next day, skim the fat off the cooled meat and broth and reserve for the masa mixture. Remove the meat from the broth and shred it by slicing it into 1-inch pieces across the grain. You can also use a food processor with the steel blade to shred the meat. Add the shredded meat to the chile sauce. Reserve the broth for the masa.

To make the wrappers, rinse the corn shucks with warm water before placing them in a large pot filled with hot water. The dried shucks tend to float to the top and it may be necessary to weight them down with a heavy lid smaller than the pot to keep them submerged. Place the pot over high heat and allow the corn shucks to come to a boil. Reduce the heat to low and cook until the husks become soft and pliable. Remove from the heat. When ready to assemble the tamales drain only a dozen or so at a time and leave the rest in the water. Don't allow the corn shucks to dry out too much.

While the corn shucks are softening, assemble a large lidded steamer pot with a steamer rack at the bottom of the pan, or place a 2 to 3-inch raised slotted platform on the bottom of the pan. Add water almost to the level of the top of the steamer rack but not so much that the tamales will sit in water.

To make the masa, warm the broth and set aside. Measure the lard and add shortening to make 1 cup if necessary. Place in a large mixing bowl and beat with an electric mixer until it has a fluffy consistency.

Place the masa harina in a large bowl and add the baking powder and salt and stir well. Add 2 cups of the masa mixture and 1 cup of the broth to the lard and beat until smooth. Continue adding the dry ingredients with the broth until all are mixed together to a smooth consistency.

At this point, make a couple of test tamales. On a drained corn shuck, spoon 3 or 4 tablespoons of the masa mixture and spread evenly over a 3 by 4 inch area. Place about 3 tablespoons of the chile sauce and meat mixture down the center of the masa. Roll the tamale over, allowing the masa to wrap around the meat filling evenly. Twist the ends and tie with strips of husk torn from the softened corn shucks to form a plump, rounded shape. Trim the edges of the corn husks and the ends of the tamale ties. For a simpler method of wrapping tamales, after rolling the corn husk around the tamales, fold the ends underneath on the seam side and place the tamale fold-side down in the steam kettle. Steam until firm, 60 to 90 minutes. Check the water level during the cooking process and add water up to the platform level to prevent the tamales from boiling dry. Taste the first tamales and adjust the seasonings with salt and pepper if necessary. Continue assembling the tamales until all the ingredients are used. Several dozen tamales can be steamed at one time. These tamales freeze well.

Makes 9 to 11 dozen tamales

See photograph, page 12.

Tamales de Elote

GREEN CORN TAMALES

Tamales, like many of the foods that we think of as Mexican, are really an American Indian dish. What southwestern cooks call "green corn tamales" are very similar to the "leaf bread" of the Iroquois and the "kneel down bread" of the Navajo. "Green corn" is young corn, when all varieties are sweet. Because of its high starch content, white field corn (the kind used to feed cattle, not the sweet corn we eat on the cob) is the variety of choice when making these tamales, but because it is not always available, a small amount of masa harina (see Appendix) is called for in most recipes. It makes the mixture easier to handle.

This recipe results in classic, delicately flavored *tamales de elote*. It comes from Danny Martinez of the Laureles Ranch, a division of the King Ranch in Texas, and was adapted from his recipe in the *King Ranch Cook Book*. For a spicier variation, add $^{1}/_{2}$ pound shredded Longhorn or Cheddar cheese and 1 peeled, seeded, and chopped Anaheim chile to the corn mixture.

4 cups fresh corn kernels (8 to 10 ears), husks and cobs reserved

½ cup lard or vegetable shortening

¼ to ⅓ cup masa harina (if not using field corn)

1 teaspoon salt

Chop the corn coarsely in a food processor using the steel blade. Add the lard, $^{1}/_{4}$ cup of the masa harina, and the salt. Pulse on and off until well blended. If the mixture seems too watery, add a little more masa harina.

To form the tamales (using the reserved corn husks), place a large green husk horizontally in front of you. Spoon 2 to 3 tablespoons of the corn mixture onto the husk about halfway between its center and the edge nearest you. Fold the edge nearest you over the filling. Then roll the tamale away from you to enclose the filling. Twist the ends and tie securely with thin strips of husk or kitchen twine.

Improvise a "rack" by placing some of the reserved corn cobs in the bottom of a large steamer, or use a pot with a rack. Arrange layers of tamales on top of the cobs, alternating the direction of each layer. Carefully pour about 3 cups of boiling water over the tamales. Cover the pot and steam for 1 hour over medium-high heat. Watch to make sure that the pot does not boil dry, and add more boiling water as needed.

Makes about 2 dozen tamales

Atole

BLUE CORNMEAL PORRIDGE

Atole is a traditional New Mexican porridge with pre-Hispanic origins made from blue cornmeal. It is one of the comfort foods of New Mexican cooking and is often served to the sick and the elderly because it is easy to digest. Honoring a long held belief that *atole* helps nursing mothers increase the flow of milk, it is still offered on the menu three times a day in the maternity ward at St. Vincent's Hospital in Santa Fe.

Serve this flavorful porridge in a colorful bowl dotted with a pat of butter and topped with hot milk and sugar. You may also do as some *vaqueros* do and sprinkle it with ground red chile or minced fresh chiles. When thinned with milk or water, *atole* is consumed as a hot drink. When chocolate is added, it is called *champurrado*.

⅛ teaspoon salt

¾ cup blue cornmeal

1 cup whole milk

Butter and sugar

In a large saucepan, bring 2 cups of water and the salt to a rolling boil. Meanwhile, mix the cornmeal with $^1/_2$ cup plus 2 tablespoons of cold water to make a soft paste. Stirring constantly with a whisk, add the cornmeal paste to the boiling water. Be very careful; the hot mixture tends to spit as you stir. Reduce the heat to low and cook the *atole* for 8 to 10 minutes, until thick.

Heat the milk in a small saucepan until it forms little bubbles around the inside edge of the pan. Divide the *atole* among 4 bowls, top each with a pat of butter and sprinkle them with sugar. Pour about $^1/_4$ cup of hot milk over each bowl and serve.

Serves 4

Chilaquiles con Carne

TORTILLA AND BEEF SKILLET BREAKFAST

The Spence family came to Mexico in 1882, as part of a group of Australian and New Zealand ranchers who bought land in the northern state of Coahuila. These were dangerous times in northern Mexico. The fierce Comanche were still actively raiding and killing settlers. Later, during the Mexican Revolution, foreign settlers were not always popular. Nevertheless, the Spences stayed on, became Mexican citizens, and are still ranching. Theirs was the first ranch to introduce the Santa Gertrudis breed, developed on the King Ranch in Texas, to Mexico.

We were fortunate enough to visit Chavela Spence Sellars—a cousin of my husband, Gordon Black—and her husband, Charlie Sellars, at their ranch, La Escondida, while doing research for this book. We had wonderful food at the ranch. One of our favorite breakfast dishes was *chilaquiles*, a traditional way to use leftovers, as prepared by Gustavo Almagues—the ranch foreman and a fantastic cook. Serve the *chilaquiles* with scrambled or fried eggs and a side of refried beans.

6 small (6-inch) corn tortillas, day old if possible

Vegetable oil, for frying

¼ cup minced onion

2 cups Carne Guisada (see page 39)

1 ¼ cups shredded mild Cheddar cheese

Preheat the oven to 350° F.

Chop or tear the tortillas into bite-size pieces. Pour ¹/₂ inch of oil into a 10- to 12-inch ovenproof cast-iron skillet and heat over medium-high heat until a strip of tortilla dipped in the oil turns golden and crisp in a few seconds. (You may also deep-fry the strips at 375° F.) Fry the tortilla pieces until golden. Using a slotted spoon, remove the fried tortillas to a baking sheet lined with paper towels to drain.

Pour out all but a thin film of oil from the skillet. Add the onion and sauté for about 1 minute. Stir in the Carne Guisada and cook, stirring, until heated through, 1 to 2 minutes. Add the tortillas and half of the cheese and toss to combine. Sprinkle the top with the remaining cheese.

Place the skillet in the oven for 10 to 15 minutes, until the cheese is melted.

Serves 4 to 6

Huevos con Machacado

EGGS SCRAMBLED WITH JERKY

The heartland of northern Mexico—the high-desert ranching country in the states of Sonora, Chihuahua, Coahuila, and Nuevo Leon—is the birthplace of American cowboy culture. Boots, blue jeans, and broad-brimmed straw hats are still the everyday work clothes for many *Nortenos* and beef is their favorite food.

Eggs scrambled with shredded beef jerky is a typical breakfast dish throughout the region. Serve with a side of refried beans sprinkled with shredded queso blanco, mozzarella, or crumbled feta, a basket of warm tortillas, and your favorite salsa.

¼ cup olive oil

1 cup chopped onion

1½ cups (about 6 ounces) finely shredded Machaca (see page 48) or beef jerky

4 ripe plum tomatoes, seeded and chopped

1 serrano or jalapeño chile, seeded and minced

8 large eggs

1 teaspoon salt

½ teaspoon ground black pepper

2 tablespoons chopped fresh cilantro (optional)

In a large skillet over medium heat, heat 3 tablespoons of the oil. Add the onion and sauté until softened, but not browned, about 2 minutes. Add the shredded beef, tomatoes, and chile. Reduce the heat to medium-low and cook, stirring occasionally, until the mixture softens slightly, 4 to 5 minutes. Remove the mixture from the skillet and set aside. Wipe out the skillet. Coat with the remaining 1 tablespoon oil and place over medium heat.

In a bowl, lightly beat the eggs with the salt and pepper. Pour the eggs into the skillet and cook, stirring until they begin to scramble, about 1 minute. Gently stir the jerky mixture into the eggs. Sprinkle with cilantro and serve.

Serves 4

Ojos De Buey

EGGS BAKED IN RED CHILE SAUCE

The Franciscan missionaries who introduced Catholicism and Spanish culture to California in the late 1700s had a profound effect on what was to become "Californio" cuisine. The padres brought with them the cooking traditions of Spain combined with those of Baja California and Sonora. *Ojos de Buey*, so called because the baked eggs reminded diners of the solemn eyes of the mission's faithful red oxen, was a dish often served for supper on Fridays and during Lent.

For modern cooks, this is an unusual and delicious dish to serve for brunch, lunch, or a light dinner. The recipe below calls for the traditional method of softening tortillas by dipping them in hot melted lard (see Appendix) and then coating them with chile sauce. For aficionados of Mexican cooking, it's worth the effort. An alternative no-fuss method is to spray the tortillas lightly with olive or vegetable oil cooking spray, wrap them in a towel, and heat them in the microwave for 30 to 40 seconds.

⅓ to ½ cup lard or vegetable oil, for frying

6 (8-inch) corn tortillas

3 cups Mission-Style Red Chile Sauce (see page 24)

12 eggs

1 cup shredded Monterey Jack or Cheddar cheese, or a mixture of the two

¾ cup sliced California black olives, well drained

Fresh oregano sprigs, for garnish (optional)

In a deep 8- to 10-inch skillet over medium-high heat, melt the lard and heat until almost smoking. Turn down the heat. Using tongs, carefully dip each tortilla into the hot lard to soften, then place it on a layer of newspaper covered with paper towels to drain. Place another layer of paper towels over the tortillas and press gently to absorb any fat.

Preheat the oven to 350° F. Lightly oil a large shallow baking or gratin dish or 6 individual gratin dishes.

In a deep 8- to 10-inch skillet, warm the chile sauce over medium heat. Pour half of the sauce into a small bowl and reserve. Using tongs, dip the softened tortillas into the remaining sauce in the skillet and arrange in a slightly overlapping layer in the prepared dish. Pour the reserved sauce over the tortillas. Break the eggs over the sauce. Place the dish in the oven and bake until the eggs are set, about 10 minutes. Remove from the oven and sprinkle with the cheese and olives. Serve garnished with sprigs of fresh oregano, if desired.

Serves 6

Mission-Style Red Chile Sauce

This traditional, old California version of red chile sauce is used in the recipe for *Ojos de Buey*. It is also a good choice when making enchiladas. The addition of vinegar and sugar makes this sauce a little different from the chile sauces of the Southwest. It freezes well and can be made in advance and kept on hand.

15 dried mild New Mexican chiles (see Mail-Order Sources)

2 garlic cloves, peeled

2 teaspoons minced fresh oregano or ¾ teaspoon
dried Mexican oregano leaves (see Mail-Order Sources)

2 tablespoons olive oil

1½ teaspoons wine vinegar

½ teaspoon sugar

¼ teaspoon salt

1 bay leaf, preferably fresh

Preheat the oven to 275° F.

Rinse the chiles and place on a baking sheet. Toast lightly for about 5 minutes, being careful not to scorch. Remove the chiles from the oven and allow them to cool. Remove and discard the stems, veins, and seeds. Place the chiles in a saucepan and add boiling water to cover. Place the lid on the pan and set aside for 20 minutes to soften.

Drain the chiles, reserving the soaking water. Using the edge of a spoon or a small knife, scrape the chile pulp from the skin. Put the pulp, 1½ cups of the soaking water, the garlic, and the oregano in a food processor or blender. Pulse on and off until the mixture is pureed.

Heat the olive oil in a large, heavy skillet over medium-low heat. Stir in the chile mixture, vinegar, sugar, and salt. Add the bay leaf and simmer the sauce, stirring frequently, until it thickens enough to coat a spoon, about 20 minutes. If a thinner sauce is desired, add a little more of the reserved soaking liquid.

Makes about 4 cups

Flour Tortillas

Bread may be the "staff of life," but in the Southwest, tortillas serve the same purpose. Esther Libby of the Circle Bar Ranch in northeastern New Mexico had a way with dough—whether it was yeast dough, pie dough, cookie dough, or tortilla dough. As she measured and mixed, the warmth and love in her hands and her heart was expressed in light, tender, tasty dishes. Her daughter, Tuda Libby Crews, remembers a busy ranch kitchen fragrant with beans and chili and Esther's tortillas. Each perfectly formed circle was rolled out and cooked on a *comal* (a heavy cast-iron griddle) minutes before the meal and served warm and fresh from a towel-covered basket that looked like a tea cozy.

3 cups unbleached all-purpose flour

2 teaspoons baking powder

1 ¼ teaspoons salt

1 ¼ teaspoons sugar

½ teaspoon baking soda

3 tablespoons lard (see Appendix)

1 ¼ cups liquid (half water and half milk or buttermilk)

Butter, honey, or preserves

Sift the flour, baking powder, salt, sugar, and baking soda into a large bowl. Cut in 2 tablespoons of the lard until the mixture resembles small peas. Add the liquids and stir until a stiff ball of dough is formed.

Place the dough on a lightly floured surface and knead about 10 times. Divide the dough into 10 to 12 portions and allow to rest about 10 minutes.

Preheat a *comal* or cast-iron griddle over high heat and, using a piece of paper towel, lightly brush the surface with some of the remaining 1 tablespoon of lard. Roll each portion of dough into a thin 6-inch circle. Place each circle on the hot griddle and cook on both sides until light brown. Brush the *comal* with additional lard between batches. Stack the tortillas inside a towel, covering them to keep warm. Serve the tortillas hot, plain or with butter, honey, or preserves.

Makes 10 to 12 6-inch tortillas

Abuelita's Chicken Soup

A Texas cowboy named Gene England arrived at the Rock Corral Ranch, near Tumacacori, Arizona, in 1931. He was a dashing and restless young man, a trick roper, who had worked as a cowboy and wrangler, and as a wildcatter in the oil fields. He was also a pilot and his airplane was his home. As the story goes, Gene England fell in love with the ranch and decided to buy it. As a down payment, he put down his airplane and a pair of pearl-handled pistols.

An old Texas trail-drive song entitled "The Wandering Cowboy" ends with "It is now I'm tired of rambling, no longer will I roam. When my pony I've unsaddled in the old corral at home." For Gene England, the Rock Corral was home. He married Judy Kibbey and settled down there. Today, the ranch belongs to their daugher, Jean England Neubauer. This Southwestern version of grandma's (*abuelita's*) chicken noodle soup is a favorite family recipe.

2 tablespoons olive oil

4 skinless boneless chicken breast halves

8 Roma tomatoes, chopped

8 cloves garlic, minced

3 cups fresh spinach, washed and shredded

1 cup fresh cilantro, minced

½ cup good quality chili powder such as Santa Cruz (see Mail-Order Sources)

8 cups chicken broth

½ cup crumbled feta cheese

⅓ pound capellini pasta (or any long, thin pasta)

⅓ cup hot sauce, such as Santa Cruz

Juice of 1 lime

Salt and ground pepper, to taste

Preheat the oven to 400° F. In a heavy skillet over medium-high heat, brown the chicken breasts in oil, about 2 minutes on each side. Combine the tomatoes, garlic, spinach, cilantro, chili powder, 2 cups of broth, and the feta in a large glass baking dish. Place the chicken in the dish and spoon the tomato mixture over it. Cover and bake for 45 minutes. Remove the chicken from baking dish with a slotted spoon. Allow it to cool, then shred it. Set the chicken aside and reserve the pan sauce.

Break the pasta into small pieces and cook it following the package directions. Drain well. Place the pasta, the remaining 6 cups of broth, the reserved pan sauce, picante sauce, lime juice, and shredded chicken in a large saucepan. Season to taste with salt and pepper. Bring the soup to a boil. Stir thoroughly and simmer for about 10 minutes. Ladle the soup into warm bowls and serve with warm flour tortillas.

Serves 4 to 6

Sopa de Queso

ARIZONA CHEESE SOUP

Most of the original Arizona vaqueros came from the bordering Mexican state of Sonora, and the Sonoran influence remains strong in the Mexican-American cooking of modern Arizona. *Sopa de queso* is a traditional specialty. It is often—but not always—a milk-based, flour-thickened cream soup with diced green chiles, vegetables, and cheese. This recipe for an interesting beef broth, tomato, and chile version was given to us by Florence Gillespie of Tucson, Arizona. She first tasted this delicious soup at the ranch of her friend and cooking mentor, Maria Luisa Salcido. People in the Southwest often use Velveeta in *sopa de queso*, because it melts beautifully.

2 tablespoons olive or vegetable oil

1 cup chopped onion

1 tablespoon unbleached all-purpose flour

1 (14½-ounce) can stewed tomatoes and green chiles, such as Spanish-style, Mexican-style, or Rotel

2 teaspoons ground New Mexican red chile or chili powder

½ teaspoon dried oregano leaves

5 cups beef broth (3 14-ounce cans)

½ pound Monterey Jack cheese, shredded

Heat the oil in a Dutch oven over medium-high heat. Add the onion and sauté for 2 to 3 minutes, until slightly softened but not browned. Add the flour and cook, stirring, for 1 minute. Add the tomatoes, chile, and oregano and stir well. Add the broth and simmer over medium-low heat for 15 minutes. Stir in the cheese and reduce the heat to low. Heat, stirring, until the cheese has melted. Serve immediately.

Serves 4 to 6

Posole de Frijoles y Chicos

BEEF, BEAN, AND CORN SOUP

Lucille C. de Baca, the widow of Phillip C. de Baca of the YNB ranch at Bueyeros, New Mexico, has a recipe for *Posole de Frijoles y Chicos* that goes back to the early Spanish settlement of this region. *Chicos* are whole kernels scraped from dried ears of corn, which can be stored for the winter. The dried corn husks are saved to wrap tamales. With pinto beans and a rich beef broth, *chicos* make a hearty and delicious one-dish meal. Serve fresh tortillas on the side.

1 cup dried pinto beans, picked through and rinsed

1 cup *chicos*, rinsed

1 onion, peeled

2 garlic cloves, peeled

3 pounds bone-in beef ribs, trimmed of fat

Salt

Fresh tortillas

Place beans and *chicos* in enough soft water (or distilled water) to cover by 4 inches and soak overnight. The next day, drain off the water and place the beans in a large, heavy nonreactive kettle with a lid. Pour in 1 quart of water and add the onion, garlic, and beef ribs. Place the kettle over medium-low heat and simmer, covered, until the beans and *chicos* are tender. If you need to add water to the bean mixture, add hot water, because cold water tends to make the beans tough. The total cooking time for well-soaked beans and *chicos* ranges from 2$^{1}/_{2}$ to 4 hours, depending on the altitude. When cooked, taste and season to taste with salt.

To cook in a pressure cooker, place the beans and *chicos* in a pressure cooker and add 1 quart of water. Do not put the lid on. Bring the water to a fast boil. Remove from the heat and place the lid on the pressure cooker and put the petcock on the lid. Allow the mixture to sit for 1 hour. (This process steams the beans and *chicos* and speeds the cooking time.) Remove the lid and pour off the remaining water.

Add 1 quart of hot water, the onion, garlic, and beef ribs. Lock the lid in place and add the petcock. Bring to high pressure over medium-high heat. Reduce the heat to medium-low and cook for 40 minutes. (Or follow the manufacturer's directions for your pressure cooker.)

Place the pressure cooker under cold running water to reduce the pressure quickly. Carefully remove the petcock to release all the steam and remove the lid. Stir the mixture carefully without disturbing the meat on the ribs. Add salt to taste. Serve in soup bowls with fresh tortillas on the side.

Serves 6

Posole

PORK AND HOMINY SOUP

"**B**ring to boil 2 quarts of whole dried corn in a gallon of water to which a cup of lime water has been added. Let soak overnight. Rinse thoroughly and remove the husks on the corn at this point. You now have *nixtamal!*" These are the old cow-camp instructions for making what most people in the United States call hominy by soaking the kernels of dried white field corn in a solution of water and slaked lime. After the husk was removed, the hominy was cooked whole—as it is in this hearty soup—or ground to make masa, a dough for tortillas or tamales. Today, most Southwestern cooks buy dried, frozen, or canned hominy.

2 tablespoons oil

2½ to 3 pounds pork, bones and fat removed, cut into small pieces

2 cups chopped onion (about 1 large onion)

3 garlic cloves, peeled and minced

2 cups dried hominy (posole)

2 (16-ounce) cans whole tomatoes

1 pound whole New Mexican green chiles, roasted, peeled, and coarsely chopped, or 2 (7-ounce) cans

2 cups cooked pinto beans or 1 (14-ounce) can, drained

1½ teaspoons salt

1 teaspoon ground cumin (optional)

Shredded Monterey Jack or Cheddar cheese (optional)

1 cup chopped fresh cilantro (optional)

Hot flour tortillas

Heat the oil in a 5-quart or larger Dutch oven over medium-high heat. Add the pork in batches (to avoid crowding) and brown on all sides, 5 to 6 minutes. Stir in the onion and garlic and cook until translucent, 2 to 3 minutes. Add 2 quarts of water and the hominy and bring to a boil. Reduce the heat to medium and cook, partly covered, for 1 to 1½ hours, until the hominy is tender.

Add the tomatoes, chiles, beans, salt, and cumin. Reduce the heat to low and simmer, uncovered, for 30 to 60 minutes, until thickened. Serve sprinkled with the cheese and cilantro, accompanied by a basket of hot flour tortillas.

Serves 10 to 12

El Pato Mexican Rice

Mexican rice is less saucy than its cousin Spanish rice. In northern Mexico, rice may be served simply along with beans as a side dish or attractively garnished and presented as a separate course. The secret in making a really good and authentic version of this dish is to fry the rice properly before adding liquid. This recipe, from Rancho El Pato in Coahuila, calls for almost as much oil as rice. But after the rice has reached an even golden-brown color, most of this oil is poured off and may be reserved for future use. This process is worth the extra effort. When liquid is stirred into the fried rice and the pot is covered, the rice pops and becomes wonderfully light and fluffy in texture.

¾ cup olive or canola oil

1 cup long-grain rice

½ cup minced onion

1 garlic clove, peeled and minced

¼ cup tomato puree

½ teaspoon salt

1 avocado, pitted, peeled, and thinly sliced

1 small red onion, peeled and thinly sliced

Heat the oil in a heavy pot or large skillet over medium heat. Add the rice and cook, stirring constantly, until golden brown, about 5 minutes. Pour the rice into a strainer placed over a bowl and drain, reserving the oil for another use. Return the rice to the pot and add the onion and garlic. Sauté for 1 to 2 minutes. Stir in 2^1/$_2$ cups of water and bring to a boil. Reduce the heat to low, cover, and simmer 15 minutes. Stir in the tomato puree and salt and cook for 5 minutes, or until the rice is tender. Serve the rice garnished with the avocado and onion slices.

Serves 4

Ranch Frijoles

Located in the northeastern corner of New Mexico, the Circle Bar Ranch is "a far piece from nowhere," with no restaurants closer than forty miles away. Visitors always planned to arrive by late morning, making sure they'd be there at dinner time. Esther Libby was known for her well-stocked larder and could whip up a delicious meal for any number of guests in less than thirty minutes. Chili con carne and frijoles remain a staple at the ranch, and Esther's beans stand out in the minds of many guests who put their boots under her table. While regional differences call for various additions such as onions, tomatoes, garlic, cumin, bay leaf, chili powder, jalapeños, or other ingredients, Esther's Ranch Frijoles are pure and honest, cowboy style. And there is nothing better than campfire-cooked Ranch Beans.

2 generous cups dried pinto beans, picked and rinsed

Soft water or distilled water, for soaking beans

½ cup diced salt pork

¼ cup tomato sauce

Salt

Place the beans in a 3-quart container and add soft water or distilled water to cover the beans by about 5 inches and soak overnight.

The next day, drain the beans and place in a large, heavy kettle with a lid. Add 8 cups of fresh water, the salt pork, and the tomato sauce. Place the kettle over medium-high heat and bring to a steady simmer. Cook the beans, checking every 20 minutes or so to make certain there is enough water. Maintain the water level at $1^1/2$ to 2 inches above the beans by adding hot water as needed (cold water tends to make the beans tough.) Total cooking time for beans that have been soaked overnight is $1^1/2$ to 2 hours at lower altitudes. At high altitudes (above 5,000 feet) allow 1 to 2 hours more. Add salt to taste and serve.

To cook in a pressure cooker, clean and rinse the beans but do not soak. Place the beans, 8 cups water, salt pork, and tomato sauce in a 3-quart pressure cooker, lock the lid in place, and put the petcock on the lid. Place the cooker over medium-high heat, bring to full pressure, and cook for 25 minutes. (Or follow the manufacturer's directions for your own pressure cooker.) Place the pressure cooker under cold running water to reduce all the pressure quickly. Carefully remove the petcock to release all the steam and then remove the lid. Stir the beans, making sure to stir the bottom of the pan, and check the moisture level. A rule of thumb at the halfway point of cooking is to have about 2 inches of water above the beans. Add hot water as needed and replace the lid securely, put the petcock on, and bring the cooker to full pressure. When at full pressure, cook the beans for another 25 minutes. Repeat the cooling process and remove the lid. Stir the beans and add salt to taste. If the liquid in the beans is too thin, simmer over low heat until thickened.

To cook over a campfire, start a hardwood fire and build up a bed of hot coals. Place the soaked beans, salt pork, tomato sauce, and salt in a 3- to 4-quart Dutch oven. Add enough water to cover the beans by 3 inches. Place or hang the Dutch oven about 10 inches above an even bed of hot coals and bring the beans to a steady simmer. Tend the fire to maintain a medium-high heat, adding hot coals as necessary. Control the heat inside the Dutch oven by raising (to lower the heat) or lowering (to increase the heat) the kettle over the hot coals. Tend carefully as the beans can scorch quickly if they become dry or if the fire gets a "hot spot." Stir the beans about every 20 minutes and make certain they are not sticking to the bottom of the Dutch oven. Keep a pot of hot water over the fire for adding to the beans. Cook the beans until tender, about $2^1/2$ to 3 hours. (Cooking time at a high altitude is about $3^1/2$ to 4 hours.) Season with salt to taste before serving.

Serves 6 to 8

Old California Chicken Enchiladas

When Mexico declared its independence from Spain on February 21, 1821, the powerful missions of California began to crumble. All California residents were automatically granted Mexican citizenship and a redistribution of mission lands to private individuals began.

Far from the central authority in Mexico City, California rancheros—like their counterparts, the *hacendados* of Northern Mexico—lived a life reminiscent of that of earlier feudal lords in Europe. With their vast holdings and plenty of Mexican and Indian vaqueros to do the work, the California dons were able to devote themselves to their favorite pastimes—horsemanship, hunting, and entertaining. During this era, cooks at the great ranchos produced lavish dishes of considerable originality and sophistication. This chicken enchilada recipe is an example of their cooking.

⅓ to ½ cup lard or vegetable oil, for frying

12 (6- to 8-inch) corn tortillas

1 recipe Rancho-Style Enchilada Sauce (see page 35)

3 cups shredded poached chicken or turkey

¼ pound Monterey Jack cheese, shredded

In a deep 8- to 9-inch skillet over medium-high heat, melt the lard and heat until almost smoking. Turn down the heat. Using tongs, carefully dip both sides of the tortillas into the hot lard to soften, then place the tortillas on layers of newspaper covered with paper towels to drain. Place another layer of paper towels over the tortillas and press gently to absorb any fat. An alternative method of softening tortillas is to spray them lightly with olive oil or vegetable oil cooking spray, wrap them in a towel, and heat them in the microwave for 30 to 40 seconds.

Preheat the oven to 350° F.

Spread a spoonful of sauce over each tortilla and place ¼ cup of the shredded chicken down the center. Roll the tortillas and arrange them, seam-side down, in a 9-by-13-inch baking dish. Spoon the remaining sauce over the enchiladas and top with the cheese. Place the pan in the oven and bake about 10 minutes, or until the cheese is melted.

Serves 4 to 6

Rancho Enchilada Sauce

Tomatoes, oranges, grapes, almonds, olives, and a wide variety of other fresh ingredients flourish in California's mild climate. Early California rancho cooking, like modern "California Cuisine," reflected that lush diversity. This enchilada sauce, with its intriguing mixture of textures and sweet, hot, and savory flavors, is as modern as it is old and is quintessentially Californian.

3 ancho chiles or 3 dried mild New Mexican red chiles
¼ cup olive oil
1½ cups chopped onion
4 garlic cloves, peeled and minced
½ cup black California olives, sliced

2 (14½-ounce) cans chopped tomatoes, undrained
⅔ cup raisins
⅓ cup blanched slivered almonds
2 teaspoons minced fresh oregano or ¾ teaspoon dried Mexican oregano leaves
1 teaspoon salt

Preheat the oven to 275° F.

Rinse the chiles and place them on a baking sheet. Toast them lightly for about 5 minutes, being careful not to scorch. Remove the chiles from the oven and allow to cool. Remove and discard the stems, veins, and seeds. Place the chiles in a saucepan and add boiling water to cover. Place the lid on the pan and set aside for 20 minutes to soften.

Place the olive oil in a large, heavy skillet over medium-low heat. Add the onion and garlic and cook slowly, stirring frequently, until lightly caramelized and golden brown, 25 to 30 minutes. When the onions are nearly caramelized, stir in the olives.

Drain the chiles and place in a food processor fitted with the steel blade or a blender. Add the tomatoes and pulse on and off until finely pureed. Press the mixture through a sieve to remove the seeds and chile skins. Return 1 cup of the tomato mixture to the food processor and add the raisins and almonds. Pulse on and off until coarsely chopped. Add the raisin-nut mixture to the tomatoes and stir to combine. Add the tomato mixture and oregano to the skillet and simmer over medium-low heat, stirring occasionally, until the sauce has thickened, about 10 minutes.

Makes about 4 cups

Wild Turkey Stew

Turkeys originated in the Americas and were first domesticated there. Before civilization encroached on their breeding grounds, and overhunting diminished their numbers, wild turkeys were found throughout Mexico and North America. On the vast ranches of north central Mexico and Texas, abundant flocks still exist—protected by ranch owners and government regulation—and wild turkey still provides a special treat for the table during hunting season. The wild turkeys at Rancho La Escondida in the mountains of Coahuila feast on acorns and berries, and they are delicious in the traditional vaquero stew that follows.

4- to 6-pound wild or domestic whole turkey breast

2 medium onions

½ head garlic (8 to 12 cloves)

Salt

2 tablespoons vegetable oil

¼ cup diced onion

2 tablespoons flour

1 cup Chile Colorado (see page 50)

1 (10¾-ounce) can tomato puree

2 garlic cloves, peeled and minced

1 teaspoon dried oregano leaves

1 teaspoon sugar

½ teaspoon ground cumin

4 diced, peeled potatoes

In a large pot, cover the turkey breast with water. Peel the onions and cut them in half. Put 3 onion halves in the pot, reserving 1 half. Add the garlic cloves, and season with salt to taste. Bring to a boil, then reduce the heat to low and poach for 3 hours. Remove the turkey, strip the meat from the carcass, and dice; set aside. Return the carcass to the pot with the broth and simmer 1 to 2 hours more, adding water as needed, to make a rich broth. Strain the broth and refrigerate overnight. Skim off any fat.

In a large skillet, heat the oil. Meanwhile, dice the reserved half onion, add to the skillet, and sauté until translucent. Stir in the flour. Add the chile, tomato puree, garlic, oregano, sugar, cumin, and 3 cups of the turkey broth.

Add the potatoes to the sauce and cook until tender, about 20 minutes. Stir in the diced turkey and simmer 10 minutes.

Serves 8 to 10

OPPOSITE: *Wild Turkey Stew and Pericos*

Pericos

VAQUERO FRIED CORN BREAD

We first tasted these delicious crisp corn bread *pericos,* or "little parrots," at Rancho La Escondida in Coahuila, Mexico. Gustavo Almagues, the ranch foreman and a fine cook, prepared a delicious dinner of wild turkey stew, *pericos,* and *atole de chocolate* in Dutch ovens over the embers from a hardwood fire. He retrieved the red-hot cast-iron pans from the fire with the original cowboy potholder, a doubled-over leg from an old pair of jeans. To make the *pericos,* Gustavo dipped a large kitchen spoon first into a bowl of water and then into the corn bread batter. He spooned a perfect oval of batter into the hot fat in the pan. Using the edge of the spoon, he made indentations like those of a seashell to spread and fan out the batter. As each batch was cooked, the golden ovals were removed to a basket lined with a napkin.

1 ½ cups yellow cornmeal
½ cup unbleached all-purpose flour (optional)
1 tablespoon baking powder
¾ teaspoon salt
¾ cup lard or vegetable shortening
⅓ cup evaporated milk powder

Preheat a Dutch oven or large, ovenproof skillet in the oven at 400° F.

In a large mixing bowl, combine the cornmeal, flour, baking powder, and salt.

Reserve 2 tablespoons of the lard. Melt the remaining lard in a skillet. Remove from the heat and stir in 1 cup of hot water and the evaporated milk. Gradually mix the liquids into the cornmeal mixture until it forms a medium-thick batter.

Remove the preheated Dutch oven from the oven and add the reserved 2 tablespoons of shortening. Dip a large kitchen spoon first in a bowl of cold water and then into the batter. Place a spoonful of the batter in the hot pan and use the edge of the spoon to spread it into a fanlike shape. Continue to place more scoops in the pan without crowding. Place the Dutch oven, uncovered, in the preheated oven and bake for 8 to 10 minutes, until the cornbread is golden brown.

Remove the *pericos* to a basket lined with a towel or napkin. If the batter thickens too much between batches, stir in a little more water.

To cook over a campfire, preheat a spider (a cast-iron frying pan with a long handle and legs) or a cast-iron skillet in the embers of a fire. Prepare the batter as directed above. Melt the reserved 2 tablespoons shortening in the preheated pan and spoon in the batter as above. Put the lid on the pan and use tongs to place more embers on top. Check after 5 minutes, and continue cooking until golden brown.

Makes 10 to 12

NOTE: As an alternative, 1 tablespoon grated onion, 2 tablespoons chopped green chiles, and ⅓ cup shredded Cheddar cheese—or any combination of these ingredients—may be added to the batter.

Gustavo's Carne Guisada

BEEF STEW

Carne guisada is a beef stew typical of the cooking of the Mexican ranching states of Coahuila and Nuevo Leon, and also across the border in Texas. This simple but tasty dish may be eaten as a main course, served with rice and beans. It is also used as a filling for tacos or burritos and in *chilaquiles*. The recipe below was given to us by Gustavo Almaques of Rancho La Escondida in Coahuila.

2 pounds lean beef, cut into 1-inch pieces

2 tablespoons vegetable oil

¾ cup chopped onion

1 to 2 minced jalapeños

2 garlic cloves, peeled and minced

2 tablespoons unbleached all-purpose flour

4 cups beef broth or water

1 teaspoon ground cumin

2 tablespoons tomato puree

1 bay leaf (optional)

Salt and ground black pepper to taste

Pat the beef dry with paper towels. In a Dutch oven or large, heavy skillet over medium-high heat, heat the oil until it just begins to smoke. Add the beef—in batches if necessary—and brown on all sides. Do not crowd the pan or the beef will not brown properly.

Stir in the onion, jalapeño, garlic, flour, and cumin and cook over medium heat until the vegetables are softened, 2 to 3 minutes.

Add the beef broth and stir. Stir in the tomato puree, add the bay leaf, and bring to a boil. Season to taste with salt and pepper. Reduce the heat to low, cover, and simmer for 1 hour. Place the lid askew and continue to simmer, stirring occasionally, until the beef is very tender, 1 to 2 hours, depending on the toughness of the meat.

Serves 4 to 6

Santa Cruz Turkey

At the Rock Corral Ranch near Tumacacori, Arizona, the holiday turkey is smoked over mesquite in an old whiskey barrel. In addition to ranching, Jean Neubauer and her family own the Santa Cruz Chili and Spice Co. The recipe below is adapted from one developed by the Arizona cook Marjel DeLauer for the companies' annual recipe contest. Rubbing the bird with red chile paste imparts delicious flavor to the meat. We also liked the spicy Mexican chorizo sausage in the cornbread stuffing.

12 pound turkey

¼ cup butter

3 tablespoons red chile paste (See Mail-Order Sources) or 2 tablespoons Chili Colorado (see page 50)

1½ cups fresh chorizo or Italian salami, sautéed and crumbled

1 cup diced onion

1 cup diced celery

2 garlic cloves, minced

1 tablespoon chili powder or New Mexican ground red chile

1 teaspoon ground cumin

1 cup lightly toasted chopped walnuts

4 cups crumbled stale corn bread

¾ cup chicken broth or water

Preheat the oven to 325° F. Rinse the turkey under cold running water and pat dry. Combine 1 tablespoon butter with 2 tablespoons chile paste. Rub the turkey inside and out with the chile mixture and set aside.

In a large skillet, melt the remaining 3 tablespoons of butter and sauté the chorizo, onion, and celery for about 3 minutes. Stir in the garlic, chili powder, and cumin. Continue to cook for 2 to 3 minutes, then add the walnuts and remove from the heat. Toss sautéed mixture lightly with corn bread and 3/4 cup chicken broth. If too dry, add a little more stock.

Loosely stuff the turkey neck and cavity with the corn bread mixture, and sew the cavities closed with kitchen twine. Cook the turkey in a smoker over mesquite following the direction for your machine and maintaining a temperature of between 325 and 350° F.

If you don't have a smoker, roast the turkey on a covered grill over indirect heat or in a preheated 325° F oven, allowing 20 to 30 minutes per pound. When done, a meat thermometer inserted in the thickest part of the thigh, but not touching the bone, should register 180° F.

Serves 8 to 10

Vaquero Chicken Stew

Miguel Gamez brought his family to Arizona from Sonora in the mid 1800s. They homesteaded near Cascabel, and the family is still on this land today. Like most early ranchers, the Gamez family raised cattle, pigs, and chickens, cultivated a big garden, and gathered wild greens, seeds, and pods to supplement their diet. In *vaquero* families, the main meal of the day was served at about 2:00 P.M. A favorite dish was a chicken stew described to us by Julie Gamez, who is married to Ramon Gamez, Miguel's grandson. Sometimes the stew's broth was served first as a soup and the chicken pieces were served as a main course with refried beans.

Purists maintain that grinding spices and herbs with a *molcajete* (mortar and pestle) gives the best and freshest flavor. If you have a mortar and pestle or a miniature food processor, by all means use it. If not, mince the garlic cloves and use ground spices.

3½ to 4 pound chicken, cut into 8 to 10 serving pieces

4 garlic cloves, peeled

1 teaspoon salt

½ teaspoon cumin seed or ¾ teaspoon ground cumin

½ teaspoon peppercorns or ½ teaspoon freshly ground black pepper

½ teaspoon dried Mexican oregano leaves (see Mail-Order Sources)

1 (14½-ounce) can stewed tomatoes and green chiles, Mexican-style, Spanish-style, or Rotel

2 large red potatoes, peeled and diced

2 large carrots, peeled and diced

1 small onion, peeled and chopped

½ cup olive oil

1 cup uncooked long-grain rice

⅓ cup chopped fresh cilantro

2 limes, cut into wedges (optional)

Place the chicken and 2 quarts of water in a large, heavy pot. Bring to a boil and skim off any foam from the top.

Meanwhile, with a mortar and pestle, grind the garlic with the salt, cumin, peppercorns, and oregano. Add the seasoning mixture to the pot and stir in tomatoes, potatoes, carrots, and onion. Bring to a boil. Reduce the heat to low and simmer, covered, for about 30 minutes.

Meanwhile, heat the oil in a large skillet over medium-low heat. Add the rice and cook, stirring often, until very lightly browned but not burned, 5 to 8 minutes. Pour the rice into a strainer placed over a bowl and reserve the oil for another use. Stir the drained rice into the stew and continue to simmer, covered, until the rice is cooked, about 30 minutes. Spoon the stew into large bowls and serve sprinkled with cilantro and lime juice, if desired.

To serve the chicken as a separate course, remove it before adding the rice. Pat it dry and brown in some of the reserved olive oil.

Serves 4 to 6

Quelites

Chuck-wagon cooks on the vast ranches of the Southwest couldn't run to the store for a head of lettuce. The vaquero diet was based largely on dishes made from beans, cornmeal, and jerky—staples that were light to carry and didn't spoil.

Wild greens were a seasonal boon to both cooks and cowboys. In spring and early summer *quelites* (*Chenopodium album*, also called "lamb's-quarters," "fat hen," and "white goosefoot"), a wild green similar to spinach and very high in nutrients, were gathered on the trail and added to the cook's pot.

Seasoned with onions and sautéed, *quelites* are a delicious, dark green vegetable compatible with most main dishes. For extra flavor season the greens with a little chile caribe (coarse-ground chile with seeds).

If suitable wild greens aren't available, cultivated spinach is a good substitute. Frozen spinach may also be used.

1 strip bacon, cut in half

1 onion, peeled and thinly sliced

1 large garlic clove, peeled and minced

¾ pound fresh lamb's-quarters or 3 large bunches fresh spinach, washed, trimmed, and drained

Salt and ground black pepper

⅛ to ¼ teaspoon coarsely ground dried red chile, such as chile caribe, or red pepper flakes, for garnish (optional)

Preheat a large, heavy skillet over medium heat. Place the bacon in the skillet and cook on both sides until crisp. Remove the bacon from the pan, chop, and set aside.

Add the onion and garlic to the hot drippings and cook until translucent and slightly golden, 3 to 4 minutes. Add the lamb's-quarters, filling the skillet, and stir until the leaves steam and shrink down. Push the cooked greens to the sides of the skillet and fill the center with more leaves. Repeat the process until all the leaves are wilted and well combined with the onions.

Add the bacon and season to taste with salt and pepper. Cook an additional minute to blend the flavors. Coarsely ground dried red chile may be stirred into the greens or sprinkled over the dish as a garnish. Serve immediately.

Serves 4

Sonoran Tacos or Burritos de Machaca

FLOUR TORTILLAS FILLED WITH BEEF JERKY

Flour tortillas are typical in the hacienda (ranch-style) cooking of Northern Mexico. In the north, with its rugged terrain and arid climate, the wide variety of ingredients grown further south were not available to the early Indian settlers. The introduction of wheat—along with cattle, sheep, and goats—by the Spaniards in the seventeenth century had a profound impact on the cooking of this region.

For vaqueros on the move today, lunch often consists of a mixture of machaca (beef jerky), beans, or whatever the cook has left over from last night's meal, wrapped in a flour tortilla. Large, thin, Sonoran-style flour tortillas make ideal wrappers for these fillings. Before the days of plastic wrap and aluminum foil, fastidious vaqueros wrapped an extra tortilla around the outside of their burritos before placing them in their saddlebags. These edible, biodegradable, outer wrappings were discarded at lunchtime—to the delight of the birds and wild animals.

MACHACA FILLING

2 cups Machaca (see page 48)

2 tablespoons olive or vegetable oil

¼ cup finely chopped onion

¼ cup chopped, roasted, and peeled fresh or canned mild green chiles

1 (14½-ounce) can diced tomatoes with liquid

2 garlic cloves, peeled and minced

8 (9- to 12-inch) flour tortillas

8 to 16 pickled jalapeño slices, to taste (optional)

1½ cups shredded mild Cheddar or Monterey Jack cheese (optional)

1 recipe Salsa Mexicana (see page 51) or 1½ cups prepared salsa

To make the filling, place the machaca in a bowl and pour in enough boiling water to cover. Allow to soak until the machaca softens, at least 30 minutes. Drain and pound in a *metate* until shredded and fluffy, or place about one-fourth of the softened machaca in a food processor with steel blade and pulse on and off until shredded. Continue to process in batches until all the machaca is shredded. Set aside.

Heat the oil in a large skillet over medium heat. Stir in the onion and sauté until softened but not browned, 2 to 3 minutes. Add the shredded machaca, chiles, tomatoes, and garlic. Cook, stirring, until the mixture comes to a simmer, about 5 minutes. Reduce the heat to low, cover, and simmer for about 10 minutes to blend the flavors.

Meanwhile, on a *comal*, griddle, or large ungreased skillet over medium heat, warm the

OPPOSITE: *Sonoran Tacos with Nopalitos Salad*

tortillas until they soften and begin to puff, 15 to 20 seconds on each side. Wrap the warm tortillas in a clean kitchen towel to keep them warm. The tortillas can also be wrapped in a towel or aluminum foil and heated in a 325° F oven for 10 to 15 minutes or in the microwave wrapped in a towel for about 60 seconds, turning the packet over halfway through the process.

Place a warm tortilla on a work surface and spoon about $1/2$ cup of the filling about halfway between the center of the tortilla and the edge near-est you. Top the filling with pickled jalapeño slices and shredded cheese. To form a soft taco, fold the edge of the tortilla nearest you over the filling, then roll the tortilla away from you to form an open-ended cylinder. To form a burrito, spoon on the filling as described above, then fold in the edges of the tortilla to your left and right. Follow with the edge nearest you, then roll up to form a cylinder that completely encloses the filling. Serve topped with the salsa.

Serves 6 to 8

Nopalitos Salad

CACTUS PADDLE SALAD

Although they appear forbidding at first glance, the many kinds of cactus that flourish in the Southwest have been the salvation of cattle ranchers on many occasions. Early settlers in Arizona learned to plant living fences of ocatillo cactus to keep livestock out of their gardens. In times of drought, ranchers throughout the west continue to burn the thorns off of cactus to make it edible for cattle.

The prickly pear cactus has clumps of oval-shaped, fleshy pads. The fruit along the rims of the pads, *tunas* (sometimes called pears), is used to make a delicious bright red jelly. The pads themselves, called nopales, are edible. When raw, they are crunchy in texture because of the water they have absorbed to stave off drought.

Fresh nopales are boiled before serving, sometimes with onion or garlic and an ear of sweet corn to sweeten them. They can be obtained, fresh or canned, at specialty food stores and in some supermarkets. If nopales are unavailable, frozen French-style green beans cooked tender-crisp make a reasonable substitute.

2 to 3 (5- to 7-inch) nopales (prickly pear cactus pads), thorns removed, or 1 (7¼-ounce) can natural cactus in salt water, drained

2 tablespoons lime juice or cider vinegar

2 teaspoons honey or sugar

½ teaspoon ground New Mexican red chile

⅓ cup sunflower or olive oil

2 to 3 ripe plum tomatoes, sliced

½ small white onion, peeled and thinly sliced

Fresh cilantro sprigs, for garnish

Rinse fresh nopales well under cold running water and examine carefully to make sure that all the tiny thorns have been removed. Trim around the edges with scissors to remove the thin layer of peel. Rinse again and cut the pads into thin strips, about ½ inch wide and 2 inches long.

Bring a pot of lightly salted water to a simmer and add the cactus strips. Simmer for about 15 minutes, until tender-crisp. Rinse under cold water and drain. If using canned nopales, rinse and drain well.

In a salad bowl, combine the lime juice, honey, chile, and oil. Add the nopale strips, tomatoes, and onion, and toss gently. Allow to marinate for at least 30 minutes before serving. Serve garnished with cilantro.

Serves 4

Machaca or Carne Seca

SONORAN BEEF JERKY

Jerky was a staple for vaquero cooks in Northern Mexico, Arizona, Texas, and California. It was a convenient way to preserve meat and was light and compact enough to carry on the trail. Jerky could be nibbled as a high-energy snack or added to a variety of other dishes to give them substance and flavor. The recipe below was given to us by an old-time Arizona vaquero named Geronimo. Traditionally, in an arid climate like that of Arizona, the *machaca* was hung on a clothesline and air-dried. Modern cooks, especially those in damp climates, usually prefer to dry their *machaca* in a dehydrator or in the oven as described below.

Several recipes in this book call for shredded jerky. Some purists insist on pounding their jerky to soften and shred it, but we have found that soaking very hard, dry jerky and then draining and shredding it in a food processor works well.

6 garlic cloves, peeled

⅓ cup lime juice

2 pounds lean beef, thinly sliced (¼ inch or less)

Put the garlic and $^1/_3$ cup water in a blender and process until pureed. Stir in the lime juice.

Place the beef in a shallow bowl and cover with the garlic mixture, turning the beef to coat all the pieces. Marinate for $1^1/_2$ hours.

Place the beef slices in a dehydrator and dehydrate at 145° F for about $3^1/_2$ hours, until the meat is almost but not totally dry. Dehydrating time will vary depending upon your dehydrator temperature, the thickness of the meat, and the humidity in the air. To dehydrate in the oven: Spread the marinated meat on a baking sheet and dry in a preheated 325° F oven for 30 to 40 minutes, turning occasionally. Jerky prepared in the oven has a softer, more roast-like texture.

When the meat is dry, store it in a resealable plastic bag at room temperature for 24 hours before refrigerating. This will allow the meat to obtain an even moisture content.

Makes about ½ pound

Cazuela

JERKY STEW

Angie Vindiola grew up on a ranch near Safford, Arizona. Her parents had come to Arizona from the state of Sonora, Mexico, before 1900. Mrs. Vindiola spoke with us at length about early ranch life in Arizona.

"When an animal was slaughtered in those days before refrigeration, most of the meat was made into jerky," Angie remembers. *Vaqueros* would dry meat of different varieties—beef, mutton, goat, or wild game such as deer and rabbit—and, in hard times, even burro. Cazuela (which means casserole in Spanish) was one of the typical dishes made with jerky. The jerky was soaked in hot water to soften, then beaten in a metate until shredded and fluffy. We were interested to try this dish and found it to be delicious—at least when made with beef! Serve with a basket of hot tortillas or biscuits.

1 pound Machaca (see page 48)

4 tablespoons olive oil

1 yellow onion, peeled and cut into eighths

2 fresh green New Mexican or Anaheim chiles, seeded and chopped

2 tablespoons unbleached all-purpose flour

Salt and ground black pepper

2 fresh tomatoes, cored and chopped

¼ cup chopped fresh cilantro

Place the machaca in a bowl and pour in enough boiling water to cover. Allow to soak until the machaca softens, at least 30 minutes. Drain and pound in a metate until shredded and fluffy, or place about one-fourth of the softened machaca in a food processor with steel blade and pulse on and off until shredded. Continue to process in batches until all the machaca is shredded. Set aside.

In a large skillet, heat the oil over medium heat. Add the onion and sauté until softened, about 5 minutes. Add the chiles and continue to cook until slightly softened, 3 to 4 minutes. Stir in the flour and machaca and cook, stirring, until slightly softened, 3 to 4 minutes. Season to taste with salt and pepper. Stir in the tomatoes and 3 cups of water. Cover and continue to cook for about 15 minutes, until the meat is tender. Stir in the cilantro and serve.

Serves 4

Chile Colorado

RED CHILE PUREE

Red chile puree, made from reconstituted dried ancho chiles or New Mexican chiles, is the base for many recipes from the "vaquero states" of northern Mexico (Coahuila and Chihuahua) and in the Mexican cooking of the southwestern United States and California. These dried chiles are increasingly available in supermarkets across the United States and can also be purchased through mail-order sources. Dried chiles have a long shelflife when stored in an airtight container. Once prepared, the chile puree may be divided into convenient portions and kept frozen until needed. There is also an excellent chile puree made from fresh New Mexico chiles sold by the Santa Cruz Chili and Spice Company, founded and owned by an old Arizona ranching family, in Tumacacori, Arizona (see Mail-Order Sources).

12 chiles anchos, pisados, or dried New Mexican red chiles

1 garlic clove, peeled and minced

¼ teaspoon ground cumin

1 teaspoon masa harina

Salt and ground black pepper

1 tablespoon olive or vegetable oil

Place the chiles in a saucepan with water to cover and bring to a boil. Simmer until softened, about 30 minutes. Drain well, peel, and remove ends and seeds. Using a mortar and pestle or a food processor, puree the chiles, adding a bit of water if necessary to thin the mixture.

Combine the garlic, cumin, and masa harina in a bowl. Gradually mix in the chile puree and enough water to make a medium-thin liquid. Season to taste with salt and pepper.

Heat the oil in a skillet over medium heat. Add the chile mixture and simmer, stirring occasionally, until the mixture begins to thicken and a lighter foam rises to the top, 3 to 4 minutes. Skim off the foam, which removes some of the heat and bitterness from the chiles. You can store the puree in the refrigerator for up to a week. It can also be frozen in usable portions.

Makes about 2 cups

NOTE: If you don't peel the softened dried chiles, you will have to put the puree through a sieve.

Salsa Mexicana

FRESH SALSA

Salsa Mexicana, also called *pico de gallo* and *salsa cruda*, is one of the most popular and versatile hot sauces in Mexican and Mexican-American cooking. It is often ground in and then served directly from a stone *molcajete* (mortar). If you don't have a *molcajete*, try a food processor and pulse it on and off until the desired texture is achieved. We prefer to leave the sauce somewhat chunky, but it's a matter of personal preference.

½ medium yellow onion, peeled

1 pound ripe fresh tomatoes, peeled and seeded

2 serrano or jalapeño chiles, seeded and finely chopped, or to taste

¼ cup minced fresh cilantro

1 tablespoon lime juice

1 to 2 tablespoons olive oil

Salt

Place the onion, tomatoes, chiles, and cilantro in a *molcajete* or food processor fitted with a metal blade. Add the lime juice, olive oil, and salt to taste. Grind or chop until the mixture is saucy but still chunky.

Allow to sit for 1 hour before serving, to blend the flavors.

Makes about 1 ½ cups

Capirotada

LENTEN BREAD PUDDING

In his fascinating book, *Eating Up the Santa Fe Trail*, western food historian Sam'l P. Arnold traces the origins of *capirotada* back to the seventh-century prophet Mohammed and to probable Moorish origins in Spain. In Catholic Spain and the New World, *capirotada* evolved into a traditional Lenten dessert.

The recipe below is an early one given to us by Julie Gamez of Benson, Arizona. Julie is married to Ramon Gamez, whose grandfather Miguel homesteaded near Cascabel, Arizona, in the mid-1800s. The Gamez family recipe contains bread, raisins, cheese, and green onions. The moisture in the pudding comes from a brown-sugar syrup made from crushed *piloncillo*, the traditional cones of brown sugar used in Mexican and Southwestern cooking. As the pudding bakes, the syrup caramelizes the top of the bread cubes, making them crunchy and delicious.

¾ cup plus 1 tablespoon butter

6 green onions, thinly sliced

2½ cups crushed *piloncillo* (see Mail-Order Sources) or firmly packed brown sugar

1 tablespoon minced fresh cilantro

1 pinch ground cloves

1 cinnamon stick

8 cups cubed day-old French bread

½ pound or more of shredded Cheddar cheese or crumbled mild goat cheese

1 cup raisins or diced dried apricots, plumped in warm water and drained

1 cup shelled piñon nuts, or chopped pecans or walnuts

1 cup heavy whipping cream (optional)

To make the syrup, place ¾ cup of the butter in a heavy saucepan over medium heat. Add the green onions and stir-fry until you can smell them cooking, but do not let them brown. Add the sugar to the pan and stir briefly. Carefully pour in 2½ cups of water and cook, stirring, until the sugar is dissolved. Add the cilantro, cloves, and cinnamon stick. Reduce the heat to medium-low and simmer the syrup gently for 5 minutes, stirring occasionally. Remove from the heat and discard the cinnamon stick.

Preheat the oven to 350° F.

Place the bread cubes on a baking sheet and brown lightly in the oven, turning to toast on all sides.

Butter a 9-by-13-inch casserole dish. Arrange half of the bread cubes in an even layer in the pan. Sprinkle half of the cheese and raisins over the bread and drizzle with half of the syrup. Repeat the layers, finishing with the syrup. Sprinkle the top of the pudding with the nuts.

Bake 30 to 40 minutes, until the top is browned and crunchy. Serve warm or at room temperature, topped with the cream, if desired.

Serves 10 to 12

Atole de Chocolate

VAQUERO CHOCOLATE PUDDING

This recipe for an old-time cattle-camp dessert was given to us by Gustavo Almagues, ranch foreman and cook at La Escondida, a lovely, remote ranch about one hundred miles from the Texas border in northern Coahuila, Mexico. Many cowboys have a sweet tooth, and this quick pudding made from cornmeal, sugar, cinnamon, cocoa, and milk or water could be prepared even in remote camps where cooks had to depend on a few staples.

3 cups whole milk, 1 (12-ounce) can evaporated milk diluted with water to make 3 cups, or water

½ cup crushed piloncillo (see Note) or firmly packed brown sugar

1 teaspoon ground cinnamon

Pinch of salt

½ cup masa harina

⅓ cup unsweetened cocoa

½ teaspoon vanilla extract (optional)

In a large saucepan, combine 2½ cups of the milk, the sugar, cinnamon, and salt. Bring to a simmer over medium heat. Meanwhile, in a small bowl, whisk together the masa harina and remaining ½ cup milk to make a thick but pourable batter. If necessary, add a bit more milk or water. Gradually add the masa mixture into the simmering milk, stirring continuously until no lumps remain, until it thickens slightly.

In another small bowl, dissolve the cocoa in 2 tablespoons of hot water. Stir the cocoa mixture and

the vanilla extract into the masa mixture and reduce the heat to low. Simmer until the pudding thickens to a creamy consistency, 8 to 10 minutes. Spoon the pudding into bowls and serve immediately, or pour into a serving bowl and allow to cool and set.

Serves 4 to 6

NOTE: Piloncillo is old-fashioned unrefined sugar formed in a hard cone with a distinctive flavor. See Mail-Order Sources.

Biscochitos

SHORTBREAD COOKIES

Biscochitos are the traditional shortbread-like cookies served at fiestas, weddings, and at Christmas throughout the Southwest and Mexico. The flavor and shape of the cookies vary from one family to another. This version, with its distinctive fleur-de-lis shape, has been passed down for seven generations by the C. de Baca family, New Mexican ranchers who trace their roots back to the conquistador Cabeza de Vaca, although it has been updated by using orange juice concentrate rather than the original orange juice. We have tasted several other variations and all are good. The Miguel Gamez family, early Arizona settlers, flavor *biscochitos* with ground cinnamon, cloves, and pineapple juice. The DeMartine family of Taos, New Mexico, adds anise seeds and brandy, but no fruit juice. One thing that most everyone agrees on is that to make an authentic *biscochito,* you must use lard.

6 cups unbleached all-purpose flour

1 tablespoon baking powder

1 teaspoon salt

1 pound pure lard (see Appendix)

1⅓ cups sugar

2 tablespoons anise seed

2 large eggs, well beaten

¼ cup thawed frozen orange juice concentrate

2 tablespoons Port wine

TOPPING

1 cup colored decorating sugar or 1½ cups granulated sugar mixed with 1 tablespoon ground cinnamon

Preheat the oven to 350° F.

Sift together 3 cups of the flour, the baking powder, and salt. Stir the flour mixture making certain the dry ingredients are well combined.

In a large mixing bowl, using an electric mixer, beat the lard until it is light and fluffy. Add the sugar and continue beating until the mixture is creamy and light. Add the anise seed and beaten eggs and beat until well combined. Add the orange juice concentrate and Port wine and mix well. Add the flour mixture to the creamed mixture. Then add

the remaining 3 cups of flour, beating it in 1 cup at a time, until the dough is stiff and forms a smooth ball.

To make the topping, mix the sugar and the cinnamon.

On a floured surface, roll the dough into a rectangle about ⅝ inch thick. Smooth the sides of the rectangle with your fingers. Using a sharp knife, cut the rectangle into 2-inch squares. Using a spatula, lift a square of dough and press the top side into the sugar and cinnamon mixture to coat

evenly. Place the squares $1^{1}/_{2}$ inches apart on a large, lightly greased cookie sheet. Use a small sharp knife to make a $^{1}/_{2}$-inch diagonal cut at each corner of the square. To form the cookies into the traditional fleur-de-lis shape, using both hands, let your thumb and index finger gently grasp the opposite ends of the square of dough and squeeze them together, forming a "petal point." While you are squeezing the cut corners, gently push the dough toward the center to thicken the formation of the fleur de lis. It is more efficient to do two

sides of all of the squares on the cookie sheet, then flip the pan $^{1}/_{4}$ around and do the other two sides of each square. The *biscochitos* should be uniform and neat looking.

Bake one cookie sheet at a time for about 13 minutes, or until light golden brown around the edges. Let the *biscochitos* set on the cookie sheet for about 5 minutes. Place on paper towels to cool completely. *Biscochitos* freeze well.

Makes about 6 dozen cookies

Natillas

CUSTARD

Isabelle Garcia—born on November 5, 1883, at her family's ranch in northeastern New Mexico—was raised in an affluent Catholic household and attended convent schools in Denver and in Missouri. This level of education was unusual for women in those times, especially from that part of the country.

Isabelle later married Fulgenicio C. de Baca of the YNB Ranch in Bueyeros, New Mexico. She raised eight children, four boys and four girls. She did not seek recognition for her contributions to the operation of the ranch, nor reward for the dedication and love that she gave freely to her family. And she was a fabulous cook. This is her recipe for *natillas*, a custard pudding of early New Mexico.

**1 quart whole milk (you may use 2 cups
evaporated milk mixed with 2 cups water)
1 cup plus 2 tablespoons sugar
⅛ teaspoon salt
4 large eggs, separated
¼ cup unbleached all-purpose flour
1 teaspoon vanilla extract
Ground cinnamon or nutmeg, for garnish**

In a large saucepan over medium heat, scald the milk by bringing it to a simmer. Remove from the heat and set aside.

In the top of a double boiler, whisk together 3 cups of the scalded milk, 1 cup of the sugar, and the salt. In a mixing bowl, whisk the egg yolks, flour, and remaining 1 cup milk to make a smooth paste. Gradually whisk the yolk mixture into the milk in the double boiler. Cook over simmering water, stirring constantly, until the custard is well thickened and easily coats a spoon. Stir in the vanilla extract and remove from the heat.

Beat the egg whites until stiff but not dry, gradually adding the remaining 2 tablespoons of sugar. Gently fold the egg whites into the hot pudding. Serve warm, with a sprinkle of cinnamon or nutmeg on the top.

Serves 6

Jiricalla

SOFT CUSTARD WITH MERINGUE TOPPING

One of the most respected sources of information about mission and rancho cooking in California is *Early California Hospitality* by Ana M. Begue de Packman, published in 1938. Mrs. Begue was a secretary of the Historical Society of Southern California and a descendent of Don Franscisco Sepulveda, owner of Rancho San Vicente. She is largely responsible for preserving the history of California's Spanish Colonial food.

Having tasted and enjoyed *jericalla*, a cup custard with almost the same name that is a typical dish in the Mexican city of Guadalajara, we were eager to try Mrs. Begue's recipe for this very different custard, which is thickened with masa harina and topped with meringue. According to Mrs. Begue, the name *jiricalla* was derived from *Come y calla* ("Eat and shut up."). The recipe that follows is our adaptation of her recipe. We liked it so much, we followed the advice of those early Californios and did as the early name suggested!

6 large eggs, separated

3 cups half-and-half

1 cup granulated sugar

½ teaspoon ground cinnamon

⅛ teaspoon ground nutmeg

⅛ teaspoon salt

½ cup masa harina

½ teaspoon vanilla extract, preferably Mexican

⅛ teaspoon cream of tartar

½ cup confectioners' sugar

Preheat the oven to 425° F.

Using an electric mixer, beat the egg yolks in a large bowl until frothy and pale yellow, about 5 minutes. Add the half-and-half, granulated sugar, cinnamon, nutmeg, and salt and mix well. Gradually whisk the masa harina into the egg mixture and continue to stir until smooth. Pour the mixture into a large heavy saucepan. Cook over low heat, stirring constantly, until the mixture thickens to a custardlike consistency. Stir in the vanilla extract. Pour into a 2-quart soufflé or baking dish.

In a clean mixing bowl and using clean beaters, beat the egg whites until frothy and add the cream of tartar. Gradually add ¼ cup of the confectioners' sugar and continue to beat until stiff peaks form. Spoon this meringue over the top of custard. Place the remaining confectioners' sugar in a flour sifter or wire strainer and evenly dust over the top of the meringue. Place in the hot oven and bake 7 to 10 minutes, or until puffed and golden brown. Serve warm.

Serves 6 to 8

THE GREAT CATTLE DRIVES AND THE OPEN RANGE

THE GREAT CATTLE DRIVES AND THE OPEN RANGE

RIDING THE OPEN RANGE atop a cow pony or herding cattle on a long and dusty trail drive are romantic scenes associated with the old-time American cowboy. But they were not very romantic to the man on horseback—they meant hard work.

The American cowboy was born in Texas, where farmers raised cattle as early as the 1830s. When the animals roamed too far, the Texans would go on "cow-hunts" to gather the cattle and bring them home to brand their offspring. On these "cow-hunts," each man carried his own grub in a canvas or cloth wallet, either tied to his saddle horn or rolled up in a slicker or overcoat tied behind the saddle cantle. This wallet usually contained pieces of cornbread or biscuits, a small amount of flour or cornmeal, some fat bacon, coffee, salt, and perhaps a little sugar.

By 1845, when the Republic of Texas was admitted to the Union as the twenty-eighth state, many Texans were already turning to cattle-raising, and they gradually adopted the tools, techniques, and methods of the *vaqueros* of Northern Mexico. They let their cattle graze in common public lands, and these grazing areas became known as the open range. "Cow-hunts" continued, but ranchers pooled their resources and helped each other. Because the hunts lasted longer, food supplies and cooking equipment were often carried on pack animals. By the 1850s, two-wheeled carts—similar to the Spanish *carretas*—were used to carry supplies in open country. In camp, each man cooked his own meals.

The Civil War changed Texas cattle-raising, because many cattlemen went off to fight for the Confederacy. When they returned home after the war, they found that their herds had been scattered far and wide by fierce winter storms in 1863 and 1864. Other cattle had been neglected by the old men and young boys charged with watching them during the war.

So the "cow-hunts" resumed, with the cattlemen pooling their efforts to locate their cattle. But the animals were so plentiful that they were worth only a dollar or two a head, provided that a buyer could be found. Some cattle-raisers sold their animals for their hides and tallow in the markets along the Texas coast. Others found buyers in New Mexico and Louisiana, and still others sought markets to the north, where the demand for cattle was greater than the supply.

In March 1866, a few Texas cattle-raisers began driving herds north across eastern Indian Territory into Kansas and Missouri and they found markets in which cattle were worth ten times what they were in Texas. As this news spread throughout Texas, more herds were driven north. By 1867, the railroad had pushed westward across Kansas from the Missouri River and had reached the sleepy settlement of Abilene, which became the first Kansas railhead cattle town.

Driving herds of cattle over long distances was nothing new for the Texans. During the late

1840s, Texans had driven herds to California, where they were sold to feed hungry miners looking for gold. Such drives took five to six months. During the 1850s, other herds were driven—in less time—to waiting markets in Missouri and Illinois.

Some of the first Texans driving cattle to Kansas may have used pack animals to carry food and supplies, but freight wagons came into use as Texas trail drives became commonplace and drovers or contractors took over the work. When modified with a chuck box mounted on the tail-end, these wagons became known as "chuck wagons," and by the time they came into common use each trail drive also had a cook, frequently called "cookie," to prepare meals for the cowboys. A trail-drive crew usually numbered eleven men, including the trail boss.

The "chuck wagon" carried the cowboy's personal gear, including bedrolls along with the cook's pots, pans, skillets, Dutch ovens, a large water barrel, plus bulk quantities of coffee, lard, molasses, flour, beans, sugar, dried fruit, and canned goods. Fresh beef and bacon were wrapped in cloth or canvas tarps.

On the trail, the cook usually prepared only breakfast and supper, using one or more Dutch ovens for steaming, boiling, browning, baking, frying, and stewing. He melted beef tallow in the flat bottoms of the cast-iron Dutch ovens to prevent food from sticking. The Dutch-oven lids often doubled as grills. Breakfast was served before dawn, and afterwards the cowboys would take cold biscuits and perhaps an onion or pickle and a piece of bacon to munch on until evening camp was made and supper was prepared.

In addition to coffee, a trail meal might include biscuits or corn bread, gravy, bacon, beef or wild game, red beans—usually spiced with onions and chili—and perhaps peach, apple, or apricot cobbler, depending upon the cook's mood. Cowboys always welcomed fruits and vegetables, and they looked forward to a town-bought meal after they delivered their herds in a cattle town.

As the settlement of Kansas progressed from east to west, the cattle trade was forced westward. Between 1867 and 1885, fifteen Kansas towns located on railroads earned the distinction of being known as cattle towns; Dodge City in southwest Kansas was the last. By that time, however, countless other Texas cattle had also been driven beyond Kansas into Colorado, Nebraska, and, by the late 1870s, into Wyoming, Dakota Territory, and Montana, as cattle ranching spread into those areas.

During the 1870s, the invention of barbed wire hastened the fencing of wide areas of the West, bringing an end to the open range. By 1890, the era of long trail drives was ending, because railroads had penetrated the cattle country of Texas as well as other cattle-raising areas on the northern plains. The open range and long trail drives gradually shifted from memories to legends, but the cuisine of the American cowboy survived and lives on.

—DAVID DARY

THE GREAT CATTLE DRIVES

Cheyenne Club Crown Roast of Pork

In 1870, Cheyenne, Wyoming, was the richest town, per capita, in the United States. Wealthy Easterners and Europeans came to Wyoming Territory because of the lure of the potential profits in grazing cattle on the open range and the romance of living a cowboy life. Finding that the hotels and eating establishments in Cheyenne were not up to their standards, twelve of these men, all members of the powerful Wyoming Stock Growers Association, formed the Cactus Club.

By the summer of 1871—at a cost of $25,000—the group had constructed a three-story, mansard-roofed, brick-and-wood building with thick carpets and hardwood floors that became known as the Cheyenne Club. The facilities included a dining room, a reading room, and a billiard room on the ground floor, with six bedrooms upstairs and a kitchen and wine cellar in the basement.

Club members were expected to observe strict decorum. Profanity and obscenity were forbidden, as was cheating at cards. No games were to be played in the clubhouse for "money's sake." Despite these rules, thousands of dollars were said to have exchanged hands in private card games in the members' rooms at night.

The Club was handsomely and comfortably furnished, with paintings by Albert Bierstadt and the seventeenth-century Dutch artist Paul Potter on its walls.

To oversee this elegant establishment, the members hired François de Prato and his wife from Ottawa, Canada. As steward, Monsieur de Prato made the club an oasis for the culture-starved sophisticates on the Prairie. The servants were well-trained and the wine cellar and larder were stocked with the finest of everything. Although beef was king, the chef—who had the reputation of producing the best food between Saint Louis and San Francisco, sometimes served a festive crown roast of pork. Pickled Peaches (see page 172), Smothered Green Beans (see page 198), and Rich Riced Potatoes (see page 151) are delicious with this pork roast.

See photograph, page 60.

5 to 6 pound crown roast of pork (allow 2 ribs per person)

Salt and freshly ground black pepper

S T U F F I N G

2 pounds bulk pork sausage

¾ cup finely chopped celery

½ cup bread crumbs, preferably fresh

⅓ cup peeled and finely chopped onion

¾ teaspoon minced fresh thyme or ¼ teaspoon dried thyme leaves

¾ teaspoon minced fresh rosemary or ¼ teaspoon dried rosemary leaves

1 teaspoon minced fresh sage or ¼ teaspoon dried crumbled sage

½ teaspoon salt

⅛ teaspoon freshly ground black pepper

2 tablespoons milk

G R A V Y

3 tablespoons unbleached all-purpose flour

2 tablespoons Port or Madeira (optional)

G A R N I S H E S

Spiced apples

Fresh herbs

Fresh fruit

Preheat the oven to 450° F.

Season the roast with salt and pepper to taste and arrange the roast with the rib ends up in a shallow roasting pan. If desired, wrap the exposed rib bones with aluminum foil to prevent burning. Place the roast on the lower-middle shelf of the oven and reduce the heat to 350° F. Roast, allowing 30 to 35 minutes per pound.

Make the stuffing while roast is cooking. In a mixing bowl, combine the sausage, celery, bread crumbs, onion, thyme, rosemary, sage, salt, and pepper. Using a wooden spoon, add enough milk to moisten the mixture slightly.

One hour before the roast is done, remove it from the oven and stuff the center with the sausage mixture. Use the back of a table knife to make decorative marks in the stuffing and return the roast to the oven for 1 hour. When done, a meat thermometer inserted in center of the stuffing should register 185° F.

Remove the roast to a serving platter and keep warm. Remove and discard the foil covering the ribs. Pour the pan juices into a large heat-proof measuring cup. Skim off ¹/₄ cup of clear drippings from the top of the juices and return them to the roasting pan. Skim off and discard any remaining fat and reserve the degreased pan juices.

Stir the flour into the drippings in the pan and cook over medium heat for 1 minute, stirring and scraping the bottom of the pan to incorporate any browned pan juices.

Add the Port and enough water to the reserved pan juices to make 2 cups of liquid. Whisk the liquid into the flour mixture and cook, stirring often, until the gravy comes to a boil and thickens. Pour the gravy through a strainer into a warmed sauce boat.

Serve the roast garnished with spiced apples, fresh herbs, and fruit, if available. If desired, cover the rib-ends with paper frills.

Serves 8 to 10

Roundup Fried Potatoes and Eggs

On long cattle drives eggs were a luxury. Chuck-wagon cooks usually packed a few dozen unwashed eggs between layers of salt and brought them along to use in cakes or puddings, but they seldom "fried up a mess of eggs" for breakfast. But on roundups where camp was made within a few days of ranch headquarters, and re-supplying it was easier, fried potatoes and eggs were a favorite cowboy breakfast.

Even in more permanent camps, chuck-wagon cooks worked very hard. Cowboys had to be ready to ride out at first light and "Cookie" was usually up preparing breakfast two to three hours earlier. To simplify his morning routine, the cook would peel and cut up his potatoes the night before and store them in a bucket of water.

Jerry Baird has been cooking for roundups and chuck-wagon cook-offs for twenty-five years. Cowboys look forward to his hearty potato- and egg-breakfasts. He varies the recipe depending on what he has on hand, sometimes throwing in some chopped jalapeños or mild green chiles. He usually serves up some biscuits or corn bread with pan gravy on the side. Jerry is used to cooking for crowds. When figuring out quantities he allows one pound of potatoes and a half-dozen eggs for every three people.

3 pounds red potatoes (4 to 6)
6 tablespoons bacon drippings (see Note)
1 large onion, peeled and chopped (1½ to 2 cups)
18 large eggs
1½ teaspoons salt
½ teaspoon freshly ground black pepper

Peel the potatoes and cut them into ³/₄-inch dice. If making ahead, store them in cold water to cover to keep them from discoloring. Drain well and pat dry with a towel before frying.

In a Dutch oven or 13- to 14-inch skillet, heat the drippings over medium-high heat. Add the potatoes and fry, stirring occasionally, for about 10 minutes, until browned and half-cooked. Add the onion and continue to cook for 8 to 10 minutes more, or until the potatoes and onion are tender. Beat the eggs with the salt and pepper. Pour the eggs into the potato mixture and cook, stirring constantly, for 5 to 6 minutes, or until the eggs are set.

Serves 9 to 10

NOTE: Three tablespoons each of butter and vegetable oil may be used in place of the bacon drippings.

See photograph, page 8.

Sourdough Starter

It's hard to imagine chuck-wagon cooking without biscuits, and for the cowboys in the days of the big trail drives of the late 1800s, biscuits meant sourdough!

Not that sourdough cooking was limited to biscuits. Cowboys also had a hankering for sourdough pancakes, sourdough bread, and sourdough cornbread.

Many modern cooks love the distinctive flavor of sourdough, but if they don't bake regularly, they are either put off or intimidated by the idea of having to feed and maintain a starter. Having killed off at least two starters that were given to me by friends, I can sympathize. In researching this book, the most convenient and fast-working recipe we have found for sourdough starter is the one preferred by the late Dick Shepherd, chuck-wagon cook for the Matador Land and Cattle Company in the Texas Panhandle. The advantage of Mr. Shepherd's starter is that it is ready to use in just twelve hours. Although you may choose to feed this one and keep it going (see Note), it is really just as easy to use it up and mix up another batch the night before you plan to bake, although purists wll say that the sour flavor needs to develop over time. The recipe below was first printed in *Chuck Wagon Recipes and Others*, a fine book about traditional and modern chuck-wagon cooking, written by Dick Shepherd's daughters, Sue Cunningham and Jean Cates (see Mail-Order Sources).

1 (1¼ ounce) package active dry yeast

¼ cup sugar

4 cups unbleached all-purpose flour

1 potato, peeled and cut into quarters

In a 1 gallon crock (see Mail-Order Sources) or large pottery bowl, dissolve the yeast in 4 cups of warm water. Allow to stand 2 to 3 minutes, then stir in the sugar. Gradually sift in the flour and stir until well combined. Add the potato and cover with clean kitchen towel. Let stand 12 hours in a warm, draft-free spot, stirring occasionally. After 12 hours it is ready to use in a recipe.

Makes 6 cups

NOTE: After using 2 cups of the starter, you will need to feed the remaining starter. Add 1 cup water, 1 cup flour, and 1 tablespoon sugar and mix well. Refrigerate until using again.

Sourdough Hotcakes

Before commercial yeast became available, one kind of sourdough starter was created from a mixture of warm potato cooking water, potato pulp, sugar, and flour. When covered loosely and placed in a warm spot, this mixture attracts wild yeast from the air and activates any yeast already present in the flour. In this nurturing environment, the yeast starts a process of fermentation and forms a sour dough.

Unlike the controlled commercial strains of yeast available today, wild yeast is unpredictable. A cook creating a starter the old-fashioned way, without adding commercial yeast, might end up with one with little rising power and an "off" flavor, or if he was lucky, it might be great. No wonder sourdough cooks treasured a good starter. Once they had it going, they took great pains to keep their starter alive and "workin'." In winter this could be a challenge, because the cold is bad for a starter and freezing may prove fatal. If the weather was cold, protective ranch cooks were known to sleep with their crock of sourdough.

Although sourdough biscuits baked up in a Dutch oven were more usual on trail drives, hotcakes were a favorite cowboy breakfast when back at the ranch. This old recipe for sourdough hotcakes came down in the Ketcham family, my ancestors who have ranched in Wyoming and northern Colorado since the mid 1800s. We think it's a good one!

½ cup Sourdough Starter (see page 67)

1 (12-ounce) can evaporated milk

1 ½ cups lukewarm spring water or distilled water

¼ cup sugar

3 cups unbleached all-purpose flour

1 teaspoon salt

1 teaspoon baking soda

The night before you plan to make the hotcakes, mix the starter, milk, water, sugar, and flour in a large nonreactive bowl to form a batter. Cover and allow to rise at room temperature for at least 12 hours.

The next morning, the batter will look creamy, with lots of holes on the top. Reserve $^{1}/_{2}$ cup to use as a starter for the next batch. Stir the salt and baking soda into the remaining batter.

Heat a lightly greased griddle or frying pan until a sprinkle of water sputters upon contact. Using $^{1}/_{3}$ cup batter for each hotcake, pour the batter onto the griddle. Cook the hotcakes until bubbles form on top. Turn and cook until lightly browned on both sides.

Makes 20 4-inch hotcakes

NOTE: If desired, a cup of blueberries, nuts, or other fruit may be gently folded into the batter before cooking.

Steve McCoy's Tomato-Maple Syrup

When I was a child, my father's uncle Will Ketcham and his friend Steve McCoy—two old-timers who had cowboyed together in the Chalk Bluffs region of northern Colorado a few miles from where I live today—had great stories to tell of roundups and of the wild days when the prairie wasn't fenced and a man could ride for miles without seeing barbed wire or opening a gate. While researching this book I ran across a fascinating journal written by a young cowboy named Leo V. Price. I'd grown up hearing that Steve McCoy was quite a cook, so I was thrilled to find an account in this journal of a roundup held in the early 1900s for which Steve did the cooking.

> There was a small two-day roundup in the early summer that ended up at Steve McCoy's. Steve was living at the old McIver place at that time....
>
> The riders were Ed and I, Steve McCoy, Harry Whole, Jack Boyle, Will Ketcham, Mr. Bud, Frank McIver, Leo Aicher, and a couple of men from Johnstown who were up visiting Steve.
>
> It was a short roundup, to get the early spring calves branded, and the cattle hadn't had time to get scattered too far over the range....
>
> We pushed the cows and calves towards Steve's ranch, and left them on the prairie out a way from Steve's. Then all in to Steve's for chow and rest for the night.
>
> The next morning we went out and brought the herd into Steve's corrals. We had 75 to 100 cows with calves and it was a big day's work roping, branding and castrating.
>
> In the evening the boys traded stories, played cards, and enjoyed the rest they had earned....
>
> I will never forget the breakfast Steve had the next morning....
>
> Steve made up a big batch of biscuits, and one thing he had which "hit the spot" for me and made me always remember that breakfast, was some tomato syrup. Something I had never had before and I thought it was the best stuff that was ever invented.
>
> He took a can of tomatoes and dumped it into the frying pan, then dumped in a lot of sugar and cooked it until it was almost preserves, and flavored it with maple. Boy, I'll never forget that treat of good biscuits and hot tomato syrup. It was worth all the hard days riding and holding down calves.
>
> —from *Pioneer Days in Gerry Valley*, by Leo V. Price

After reading Leo Price's description, I was eager to try that tomato syrup. I got in touch with Steve's granddaughter, Sylvia McCoy Childers, and, although Steve wasn't one to write down a recipe, together we have tried to re-create it. Be sure to serve it with hot biscuits.

1 (28-ounce) can tomatoes, undrained

¾ cup sugar

¼ cup maple syrup

In a large skillet, combine the tomatoes and sugar. Cook, stirring, over medium heat until the sugar is dissolved. Add the syrup and cook, stirring frequently, for about 30 minutes, until the mixture thickens to the consistency of preserves.

Makes about 1½ cups

Sourdough Corn Bread

Sourdough corn bread unites the corn bread of South Texas and the sourdough of the High Plains. Texas cowboys and chuck-wagon cooks developed a taste for sourdough on cattle drives to the northern ranges of Wyoming, Montana, and the Dakotas. Eventually, as often happens when people travel, sourdough spread south and was incorporated into corn bread.

This Sourdough Corn Bread recipe comes from Carl Cooper of the Hitch Ranch in the Oklahoma Panhandle.

1 cup Sourdough Starter (see page 67)

2 cups cornmeal

1½ cups milk

¼ cup sugar

2 large eggs, beaten

¼ cup warm melted butter or vegetable shortening

1 teaspoon salt

½ teaspoon baking soda

Preheat the oven to 425° F. Grease an 8- to 10-inch ovenproof skillet or Dutch oven.

In a large mixing bowl, combine the sourdough starter, cornmeal, milk, sugar, and eggs. Stir in the melted butter, salt, and baking soda. Pour the batter into the prepared pan and bake 25 to 30 minutes, until the corn bread is golden on top and a toothpick inserted in the center comes out clean.

Serves 6

Cowboy Coffee

Cowboys liked their coffee strong, black, and plentiful. To satisfy their thirst, most ranch cooks kept a two- to five-gallon pot of coffee brewing at all times. Although early cooks roasted their own beans, by the 1870s many cattle outfits were buying preroasted beans in bulk from Arbuckle Brothers of Pittsburgh, Pennsylvania. The Arbuckles developed a method of coating roasted coffee beans with a mixture of egg white and sugar to prevent oxidation and help preserve the fresh-roasted flavor. Arbuckle coffee was sold in 100-pound burlap bags containing one hundred one-pound packages wrapped in brown paper. Included in each package was a stick of peppermint candy, which was customarily given to the cowboy who helped "Cookie" grind the beans.

Old-fashioned cowboy coffee is boiled. Some ranch cooks insist that you can't make decent coffee without adding a raw egg—or at least an eggshell—to the pot.

We have tried making coffee with and without the egg and find that if the coffee beans and the water are of good quality, both methods produce a good brew. Adding an egg or eggshell does make a clearer looking cup of coffee, because it acts as a magnet for sediment and helps to settle the grounds.

In his book *Eating Up the Santa Fe Trail*, our friend Sam'l P. Arnold includes an excellent historic recipe for making campfire coffee with an egg. We have asked Sam's permission to borrow his recipe. The coffee is, as Sam claims, "absolutely superb." Our eggless version comes from Will Ketcham, Steve McCoy, and many other old cowboys who could make good coffee in a tin cup. When necessary, cowboys brewed coffee directly in their large tin coffee cups. If making coffee in the cup, sip it carefully, or you will end up with a mouthful of grounds!

Sam'l P. Arnold's Campfire Coffee

1 cup ground roasted coffee

1 large egg

½ cup cold water

In a coffee pot, bring 2 quarts of cold water to a boil. Allow to boil only 2 to 3 minutes. Meanwhile, place the coffee and egg in the sack. Break the egg in a clean cotton sack and mix it with the coffee by massaging the bag. Drop the sack into the boiling water and cook for 4 minutes. Remove the pot from heat and pour in ¹/₂ cup cold water to settle the grounds.

Makes about 8 cups

No Frills Cowboy Coffee

1 to 1½ cups ground roasted coffee

Place the coffee in an old-fashioned 2-quart coffee pot and fill with cold water. Bring to a boil and simmer for 2 minutes. Remove from the fire or heat and pour in 1 cup of cold water to settle the grounds. Let sit for 2 minutes and carefully pour the coffee into cups to avoid stirring up the grounds.

Makes about 8 cups

Biscuits on a Stick

Before the days of big roundups and trail drives of the late 1800s, cowboys often cooked for themselves. During the spring and fall roundups, small groups fanned out in different directions to hunt for cattle. Unless they planned to be away for more than a week, most preferred to travel without a pack animal. Each man stashed his provisions in a double-sided canvas saddlebag called a "wallet" and packed it on his saddle horse. Rations usually included hardtack or leftover bread and biscuits, a small sack of parched corn flour or wheat flour, coffee, a little salt, saleratus (baking soda), a tin of lard, and a chunk of bacon or salt pork. They mixed up biscuit dough in a flour sack and cooked both biscuits and meat on green sticks over the campfire. The two recipes that follow are more modern ranch recipes, adapted to the old-time cooking method.

Arizona Oatmeal Biscuits

1 ½ cups unbleached all-purpose flour

¾ cup quick oats

1 tablespoon baking powder

1 teaspoon salt

½ cup chilled lard or vegetable shortening

½ cup shredded Monterey Jack cheese with jalapeño peppers (optional)

½ to ¾ cup cold milk

Texas Chile-Cheese Biscuits

2 cups unbleached all-purpose flour

1 tablespoon baking powder

1 tablespoon ground New Mexican red chiles or chili powder

1 teaspoon salt

½ cup chilled lard or vegetable shortening

½ cup shredded Cheddar cheese

¾ cup cold milk

To make either flavor of biscuits, combine the dry ingredients in a mixing bowl. Cut the shortening into the dry ingredients with a pastry blender or your fingertips until the mixture resembles coarse crumbs. Stir in the cheese. Make a well in the center of this mixture and pour in ½ cup of the milk. Stir with a fork for about 30 seconds, until the dough begins to come away from the sides of the bowl. If the dough seems too dry to hold together, stir in a little more milk, 1 tablespoon at a time. Turn the dough out onto a lightly floured surface and knead gently and quickly for about 30 seconds, making 8 to 10 folds.

To toast the biscuits on a stick, divide the dough into 10 to 12 biscuit-size portions. Flatten a chunk of dough between your hands and form it into a tubular shape around a smooth green branch about ½ inch in diameter and 2 to 3 feet long. Don't cover the very end of the stick, as you want to be able to slip off the biscuit and fill it with butter and maybe jam. Toast the biscuits over the hot embers of a campfire or over medium-hot coals in a barbecue grill for 8 to 10 minutes, until golden brown on all sides.

To bake the biscuits in the oven, preheat the oven to 450° F. On a lightly floured board, pat out the dough to a thickness of about ½ inch. Cut out the biscuits with a glass or a biscuit cutter about 3 inches in diameter. Bake in the oven for 12 to 15 minutes, until golden brown.

Each recipe makes about 12 biscuits

Howard and La Verne Rogers' Sourdough-Buttermilk Biscuits

For the last twenty years, Howard Rogers has been the foreman and head chuck-wagon cook of the Brooks Ranch near Sweetwater, Texas. Cooking over mesquite coals, Howard expertly utilizes cast-iron cookware to prepare sourdough biscuits, pinto beans, fruit cobblers, bread puddings, and a variety of beef dishes.

Howard is known as a great Dutch-oven bread baker, but his wife LaVerne does most of the baking at home. They share the same biscuit-dough recipe but have different philosophies on the forming and baking of biscuits.

Using the traditional old cowboy technique, Howard pinches off pieces of kneaded dough and rolls them into balls with oiled hands. LaVerne prefers to roll out her dough and cut out the biscuits with a biscuit cutter (she actually uses a clean snuff can to cut the biscuits) and bakes them in a conventional oven.

Howard Rogers prefers to "hang" his biscuits instead of placing the Dutch oven directly on the coals, as some cooks do. Suspending the oven from hooks of different lengths, he achieves that "just right" temperature needed to bake the biscuit bottoms without burning them. My friend Tuda Crews, a fine Wyoming chuck-wagon cook, places the Dutch oven on a baking rack over an even layer of hot embers. Tuda suggests that novice Dutch-oven cooks may find it helpful to place an oven thermometer in the Dutch oven.

To brown the tops of the biscuits, live glowing coals are placed uniformly on the top of the oven lid. The lip of the lid keeps the coals from rolling off. Dutch-oven bread baking requires patience and frequent inspections to prevent burning. Experienced cooks use a pot hook to remove a lid loaded with hot coals without getting a nasty burn. Pot hooks, or *ganchos* ("hooks" in Spanish), are long-handled implements similar to fireplace pokers that may be fashioned from iron, steel, twisted wire, or green wood. When lifting the lid, care is always taken to prevent hot coals from falling into the biscuits, but Howard grins and admits that a few ashes add to the flavor and authenticity of chuck-wagon cooking.

1 cup plus 2-4 tablespoons unbleached all-purpose flour

2 teaspoons baking powder

1 teaspoon salt

½ teaspoon baking soda

1 cup Sourdough Starter (see page 67)

¼ cup buttermilk

3 tablespoons cooking oil or melted vegetable shortening

In a large bowl, combine 1 cup of the flour, the baking powder, salt, and baking soda. Make a well in the center and add the starter, buttermilk, and oil. Mix with a fork to form a stiff dough.

Sprinkle your work surface with 2 to 4 tablespoons of flour. Scrape the dough onto the floured surface and knead briefly until smooth. The dough will be sticky. Do not overwork.

To make the biscuits using a conventional oven, use LaVerne's method. Roll out the dough until about ¹/₂-inch thick. Cut the biscuits using a 3-inch biscuit cutter and place about 2 inches apart on a baking sheet. Cover the biscuits with a clean towel and set them aside in a warm place to rise for about 30 minutes, until about doubled in size. Preheat the oven to 425° F. Bake for about 20 minutes, until golden brown.

To cook over a campfire, use Howard's method. Pinch off golf-ball size pieces of the kneaded dough with oiled hands and place close together in a well-oiled Dutch oven. Cover with a towel to rise for about 30 minutes. While the biscuits are rising, place the lid in the fire to preheat. Either suspend the Dutch oven above the coals or place it on a baking rack over an even layer of hot embers or a circle made up of about 24 hot coals. Place an oven thermometer in the Dutch oven. (While cooking the biscuits, try to maintain an even temperature of between 400° and 425° F.) Carefully lift the oven lid from the fire with a pot hook and tap it against a shovel to jar off any clinging ash. Carefully place the lid on the Dutch oven and use tongs to cover it with an even layer of live coals. Cook the biscuits until golden brown, about 15 minutes, checking frequently.

Makes 12 to 15 biscuits

Trail Drive and Bunkhouse Milk Gravy

Milk cans and tins that once held baking powder, found in the unsightly but interesting trash dumps around old ranches and homesteads, are testimony to the cowboy taste for biscuits 'n gravy. On the trail or at home, a milk gravy was usually served with biscuits, made with bacon drippings or lard, if pan drippings were not available. The cows that early cowboys herded were not of the milking variety—they were mostly cantankerous Longhorns—and, in any case, cowboys don't want to milk cows! For most cowboys, at least on cattle drives, milk was something that came in a can.

2 tablespoons meat drippings, bacon drippings, or lard

3 tablespoons unbleached all-purpose flour

1 (12-ounce) can evaporated milk

Salt and ground black pepper

In a large skillet, heat the drippings over medium heat. Stir in the flour and cook for 2 to 3 minutes, until the flour turns golden. Add the milk and half a can of water. Cook, stirring, until the gravy is smooth and thickened. Season to taste with salt and pepper and serve over biscuits.

Makes about 2 cups

Cowboy Frying-Pan Bread

When camping out, High Plains cowboys like my father's uncle Will Ketcham often made a skillet biscuit-bread similar to the bannock favored by early trappers and mountain men. The dough was mixed up right in the flour sack and cooked in a lightweight, long-handled camp skillet over an open fire. After a crust formed on the bottom, handy cooks propped up the skillet in a nearly vertical position, with the top of the bread facing the fire, to allow the loaf to rise and brown on top.

We have tried this campfire baking technique and find that if you are careful, the bottom crust keeps the bread from sliding out of the pan and into the fire or dirt. Although flipping the bread to brown the bottom might seem like a good alternative, we don't recommend it because you will end up with a heavy pancake instead of a light, crusty loaf.

2 cups unbleached all-purpose flour

3 teaspoons baking powder (use 2½ teaspoons at high altitudes)

1½ teaspoons salt

1 teaspoon sugar

6 tablespoons lard or vegetable shortening

Butter and jam for serving

Preheat the oven to 425° F.

In a mixing bowl, combine the flour, baking powder, salt, and sugar and mix thoroughly. Make a well in the dry ingredients. Place the shortening in a 9- or 10-inch ovenproof skillet and melt over medium-low heat. Swirl the shortening around in the skillet to coat it thoroughly. Pour the remaining shortening into the well in the dry ingredients. Using a fork, stir the shortening into the dry ingredients until the mixture resembles peas. Pour in ⅔ cup of water and continue to stir for about 30 seconds, until the dough starts to come away from the sides of the bowl. Don't be concerned if the mixture seems lumpy. That's how it should look.

Turn the dough out onto a lightly floured surface and knead it for about 30 seconds. The dough should be slightly sticky. Press the dough into the greased skillet in an even layer. With the end of a knife or spoon handle, poke a hole about the size of your thumb in the center of the loaf to allow steam to escape and permit the bread to bake evenly.

Place the skillet on the bottom shelf of the oven for 10 minutes, until the bottom of the loaf is lightly browned and the loaf has stiffened. Move the skillet to the upper third of the oven and bake for 15 to 20 minutes, until the top of the loaf is golden brown.

To bake over a campfire, place a cast-iron skillet filled with the dough on the hot embers for 5 to 10 minutes, then prop the skillet in a nearly vertical position and carefully rotate the pan to brown the top of the bread evenly for 15 to 20 minutes.

Brush off any ashes, cut the bread into wedges, and serve with butter and jam.

Serves 4 to 6

Jerry Baird's Texas Corn Bread

In the early days of ranching, before Texas cowboys moved longhorns up the trail to Kansas and beyond, corn bread was their everyday fare. The years following the Civil War were hard for Texans. Cornmeal, or "yaller bread" as it was called, was more available and much less expensive than wheat flour. White bread and biscuits, at that time, were served only on special occasions and savored almost like cake. Prosperity has returned to Texas and more biscuits are served, but corn bread has held its place in the hearts of Texas cowboys.

Jerry Baird is a Texas rancher and long-time chuck-wagon cook. In 1995, his wagon was one of those selected to cook for the start of the Longhorn Cattle Drive from Texas to Montana. He bakes great old-fashioned corn bread in a Dutch oven over hot embers from an open fire. One secret to making good corn bread is to have your Dutch oven well greased and preheated before pouring in the batter. When asked how many embers or hot coals to use when baking corn bread, Jerry says his rule of thumb is "six on the bottom and load up the top." (For more information about Dutch-oven bread baking, see Howard and LaVerne Rogers' Sourdough Biscuit recipe on page 74.) If he needs corn bread in a hurry, Jerry spoons pancake-size portions of the batter into a hot, well-greased skillet and fries it until golden brown.

¼ cup plus 1 ½ tablespoons bacon drippings or vegetable oil

1 cup yellow cornmeal

1 cup unbleached all-purpose flour

¼ cup sugar

1 tablespoon baking powder

½ teaspoon salt

1 cup milk or reconstituted evaporated milk

2 large eggs

To bake in a conventional oven, place 1 ½ tablespoons of the drippings or oil in an 8-inch-square baking pan. Tilt and turn the pan to coat the sides and place in the oven. Preheat the oven to 400° F.

In a mixing bowl, combine the cornmeal, flour, sugar, baking powder, and salt. Stir in the milk, eggs, and remaining ¼ cup drippings and blend well. Spoon the batter into the preheated pan and bake for about 20 minutes, until the bread is golden brown and a knife inserted in the center comes out clean. Cut into squares and serve.

To bake over a campfire, put 1 ½ tablespoons of the drippings in a 10- to 12-inch Dutch oven and place both the oven and its lid over the embers to preheat while preparing the batter. Pour the batter into the preheated Dutch oven and, using a pot hook, carefully place the hot lid on top. Using long-handled tongs, arrange an even layer of embers on top of the lid. Cook the bread 15 to 20 minutes, until golden brown, checking frequently.

Serves 6 to 8

Dorcie's Corn Cakes

During the cowboy era in south and east Texas, cornmeal was more widely available than wheat flour. So cowboys ate a lot of corn bread. Corn pones, corn dodgers, or hoecakes—fried in a skillet or baked in the embers of the campfire—were simple breads that a cow hunter could throw together quickly. Leftovers were packed in his saddlebag for trail food. At ranch headquarters, or on trail drives where a cook and chuck wagon accompanied the crew, lighter, more elaborate corn breads made with eggs and milk were a welcome treat.

This old-fashioned corn cake recipe comes from Guy and Pipp Gillette's mother, Doris Porter Gillette, who remembers her mother and grandmother preparing this dish. They made one large cake the size of the skillet and served it cut into wedges. Mrs. Gillette finds that individual cakes are easier to turn and brown on both sides. They go well with chili and are great for breakfast, served with bacon and eggs or topped with butter and syrup.

2 cups yellow cornmeal

½ cup unbleached all-purpose flour

2 teaspoons salt

2 tablespoons corn oil

In a mixing bowl, combine the cornmeal, flour, and salt. Stir in 2 cups of boiling water and form the mixture into 10 to 12 patties.

Heat the oil in a large skillet over medium-high heat. Fry the patties 3 to 5 minutes on each side, until well browned.

Serves 4 to 6

Muleskinner's Chili

The origins of chili con carne lie in the *guisadas* (chile-flavored stews) of northern Mexico. Many cooks on cattle drives were Mexican. They cooked and seasoned their beef or pork stews as they always had—with chile, cumin, onions, garlic, and tomatoes. Pinto or red beans were served with these stews as a side dish.

The cowboys who followed the Longhorns up the trails from Texas came from diverse ethnic backgrounds. Black, white, Mexican, and American Indian cowboys often rode together, eating the same food and sharing the same jobs and dangers. Even those who hadn't grown up eating spicy food developed a taste for chili.

Over the years chili con carne has evolved into many different versions and become an American passion. Chili cook-offs are held on a state, national, and even international level, and competition is fierce. Aside from the use of chiles as a seasoning, some of the recipes have ranged pretty far from the original chuck-wagon fare with additions of exotic ingredients like crumbled gingersnaps and mango chutney.

Almost every ranching family in Texas has its favorite chili recipe, many of which have been handed down for several generations. The Gillettes of Crockett, Texas—brothers Guy and Pipp, and Guy's wife Cathi, who is also an accomplished chuck-wagon pot wrastler—compete in, and have won, many traditional chuck-wagon cooking competitions. Entrants are judged both on their cooking skills and on the authenticity of their wagon. The Gillettes' wagon, with its matched team of white mules, is a standout. Their chili—cubed beef and pork, with beans served on the side—is reminiscent of early Texas and New Mexican recipes. It is a chili with authority; delicious but hot. Tenderfeet may wish to cut back a little on the chiles and forgo the cayenne. Serve it with Chuck-Wagon Beans (page 82) and Dorcie's Corn Cakes (page 78).

2 strips thick-sliced bacon

1 pound boneless pork chops, cubed

1 pound round steak, cubed

1 pound ground round steak

2 yellow onions, peeled and chopped (about 2 ½ cups)

3 garlic cloves, peeled and minced

1 (10-ounce) can Rotel tomatoes or Mexican- or Spanish-style tomatoes with green chiles

1 (8-ounce) can tomato sauce

2-4 dried ancho chiles, chopped, or ¼-½ teaspoon crushed red pepper

1 teaspoon Tabasco sauce

3 heaping tablespoons chili powder

1 tablespoon ground cumin

1 tablespoon dried oregano leaves

¼ teaspoon ground oregano

2 teaspoons cocoa powder

1 ½ teaspoons salt

1 teaspoon paprika

¼ teaspoon cayenne pepper

12 ounces beer

In a large, heavy skillet over medium-low heat, cook the bacon, turning occasionally, until crisp, about 5 minutes. Remove the bacon, crumble, and set aside. Pat the meat cubes dry with paper towels. Brown the cubed meat and ground meat in the bacon drippings. If the skillet isn't large enough, brown the meat in batches to avoid crowding. Transfer the browned meat and any juices to a Dutch oven.

In the same skillet, sauté the onion and garlic for 2 to 3 minutes over medium heat, until slightly softened, adding some bacon drippings or oil to the pan, if necessary. Transfer the onion mixture to the Dutch oven and add the reserved bacon, tomatoes, tomato sauce, chopped chiles, and Tabasco. Bring the mixture to a simmer over medium-high heat, stirring to combine well. Reduce the heat to low, cover, and cook gently for 30 minutes. Add the chili powder, cumin, oreganos, cocoa, salt, paprika, and cayenne. Stir in the beer. Cover and cook over low heat for 2 hours, stirring occasionally, until the chili has thickened and the meat is tender.

Serves 8 to 10

OPPOSITE: *Muleskinner's Chili, Dorcie's Corn Cakes, and Chuck-Wagon Beans*

Chuck-Wagon Beans

Guy and Pipp Gillette spent 15 years touring the United States and Europe as professional musicians before settling down to run the Texas ranch their grandfather, H. V. "Hoyt" Porter, purchased in 1912. Both brothers are interested in cowboy culture and traditions. They have restored the 1920s-style houses on the ranch and built a central, old-fashioned "cook shack," patterned on the one at the Lambshead Ranch near Albany, Texas. In addition to operating their cattle business, Guy and Pipp continue to be involved with music. They just released their second cassette, *Cinch Up Your Riggin'*, a collection of cowboy songs (To order, write or call the Gillette Ranch, Rt. 4, Box 131, Crockett, Texas 75835; (409) 636-7165). The brothers are avid chuck-wagon cooks who take their vintage wagon to competitions and exhibitions all over the Southwest. This is their recipe for Chuck-Wagon Beans. For more information on cooking beans in a pressure cooker or over an open fire, see the recipe for Ranch Frijoles (page 32).

1 pound dried pinto beans, picked over and rinsed

Soft water or spring water, for soaking

4 strips thick-sliced bacon, chopped

2 cloves garlic, peeled and minced

1 teaspoon sugar

Salt

Soak the beans in soft water or spring water overnight.

In a Dutch oven over medium heat, cook the bacon until crisp, 3 to 4 minutes. Add the minced garlic to the pan and sauté for about 1 minute, until lightly browned.

Drain and rinse the beans and add to the bacon.

Pour in enough water to cover the beans by 3 inches and bring to a boil over high heat. Reduce the heat to low. Cover and simmer for 2 to 3 hours, stirring occasionally, until the beans are tender. Add the sugar and salt to taste and continue to cook, uncovered, for 20 to 30 minutes to reduce the liquid.

Serves 8 to 10

Carl Cooper's Oklahoma Cowboy Stew

As settlers moved to the frontier, the cowboy diet of beef, bacon, beans, and biscuits began to change. Homesteaders planted gardens for their own use; their produce was also sold or bartered. Chuck-wagon cooks broke the monotony of trail-drive cuisine by exchanging beef for sturdy vegetables such as onions, potatoes, carrots, and cabbage.

This stew comes from Carl Cooper, cattle foreman and head chuck-wagon cook for the famous Hitch Ranch of Oklahoma.

6 strips thick-sliced bacon, coarsely chopped

2 pounds beef stew meat, cut into 1-inch cubes

4 large red potatoes, peeled and cubed

6 carrots, peeled and cut into 1-inch lengths

1 large onion, peeled and chopped

1 small cabbage (about 1 pound), coarsely chopped

1 (11-ounce) can corn

Salt and ground black pepper

In a Dutch oven over medium-low heat, cook the bacon, turning occasionally, for about 5 minutes, until crisp. Remove the bacon with a slotted spoon and set aside. Pat the beef cubes dry with paper towels and add to the bacon drippings in the pan. Cook the meat over medium-high heat for 6 to 8 minutes, until browned. If necessary, brown the meat in batches to avoid crowding the pan. Add enough water to the pan to cover the meat by 1 inch. Bring to a boil, then reduce the heat to low and simmer for $1^1/_4$ hours. Add the potatoes, carrots, and onion and cook for another 30 minutes. Stir in the cabbage and corn and cook 15 minutes longer, until the meat and vegetables are tender. Season to taste with salt and pepper and serve.

Serves 6 to 8

Paul Hudman's Texas Beef Pot Roast

Paul Hudman, Sr.—a pharmacist in San Angelo, Texas—was a cowboy at heart. His love for horses prompted him to buy two pieces of land near Miles, Texas. There he spent years raising and selling registered quarterhorses. After his death in 1963, his widow kept one tract of land and sold the other place and all of the horses.

At the time, Paul, Jr., was a student at Texas A & M Veterinary School. In 1981, after several years of practicing veterinary medicine, Paul purchased the family land. Over the years, he and his son have built up their 3 H Ranch to 760 acres.

Like his father before him, Paul Hudman is a cowboy. He has a 100-year-old chuck wagon from which comes some of the best authentic "Old West" cooking you've ever tasted. Now and then he enters a chuck-wagon cook-off and has won several. This is his recipe for pot roast, which Paul often serves with a side dish of sautéed cabbage and apples (see page 85), two chuck-wagon staples.

½ cup vegetable shortening

8 to 10 pound pot roast (chuck or rump)

Salt and ground black pepper

½ cup flour

1 medium onion, peeled and cut into 8 pieces

8 baking potatoes, peeled and cut into 6 to 8 pieces

6 carrots, peeled and cut into pieces

2 cloves garlic, peeled and thinly sliced

To cook over a campfire, set a deep 16-inch Dutch oven with a flanged lid on the coals and heat the vegetable shortening. (Heat over medium-high heat if cooking on the stove top.) Rub the roast with salt, pepper, and ¼ cup of the flour. Brown the roast on all sides in the hot grease, turning several times. After browning, position the roast in the Dutch oven with the fat side up. Place the onion, potatoes, carrots, and garlic around the beef. Season with salt and pepper again, to taste. This ensures a good, rich gravy. Add enough hot water to have about an inch of water in the Dutch oven. Cover and place some coals on top of the lid and cook for about 4 hours, until the meat is tender, turning the oven a half turn every 15 minutes. At the same time, turn the lid a half turn in the opposite direction. This will ensure the roast is cooked evenly.

Remove the roast and vegetables to a serving platter and keep warm. Place the remaining flour in a small bowl and gradually whisk in ½ cup cold water. Gradually whisk the flour mixture into the simmering pan juices in the Dutch oven, stirring constantly, until the gravy is smooth and thickened, 2 to 3 minutes.

To cook in a conventional oven, preheat the oven to 300° F. Brown the roast as described above in a Dutch oven on the stove top over medium-high heat. Add the vegetables and water as above and cover. Roast 4 hours, until very tender. Remove the roast and the vegetables and simmer the juices on the stove top to make the gravy.

Serves 12 to 15

Note: If the only roast available is tough, soak it in a solution of half vinegar and half water for an hour ahead of time. Drain well before preparing the roast. For smaller groups buy a 5- to 6-pound roast and halve the other ingredients in the recipe.

Chuck-Wagon Cabbage and Apples

This recipe from Paul Hudman makes a colorful and tasty side dish for pot roast.

2 tablespoons bacon drippings or vegetable shortening

1 medium onion, peeled and finely chopped

1 head red cabbage, cut into small pieces

3 tart apples, unpeeled, cored, and cut into 2-inch pieces

1 tablespoon lemon juice

1½ tablespoons sugar

½ teaspoon salt

Heat the bacon drippings in a 12-inch cast-iron Dutch oven over medium heat on the stove top or a fire or hot coals. Add the onion and cabbage. Cook, covered, over just enough heat to steam the cabbage for 25 to 30 minutes, or until it is tender. Stir occasionally to keep the onion from browning too much.

Stir in the apples, lemon juice, sugar, and salt. Cover and continue to cook over low heat for another 25 to 30 minutes, stirring occasionally, until the apples are soft and cooked down.

Serves 10 to 12

Sourdough Batter-Fried Steak

The best way to keep a good sourdough starter "workin'" is to use some of it regularly—at least every few days—and to replace what you used with a mixture of flour, warm water, and sugar. Keeping the starter going was a challenge in isolated line camps, where one or two men spent months living in close quarters and riding the boundaries of their range. Bread or biscuits were always on the menu, but the cook had to be creative to use up that sourdough. Sourdough starter found its way into pancake batter, cobblers, and pie crusts, and was used as a coating when frying up a steak. As is often the case, necessity brought about the invention of some great dishes. Serve Sourdough Batter-Fried Steak with Trail Drive and Bunkhouse Milk Gravy (see page 75).

3 pounds elk, deer, buffalo, or beef round steak, 1 inch thick

1 cup unbleached all-purpose flour

2 teaspoons paprika

1 teaspoon coarsely ground black pepper

Salt

3 tablespoons minced onion

1 cup Sourdough Starter (see page 67)

¾ cup lard or vegetable shortening

Using a meat tenderizing mallet, pound the steak to a $^1/_2$-inch thickness and cut it into 6 to 8 pieces.

Combine the flour, paprika, and pepper, and season with salt to taste.

Stir the onion into the sourdough starter and dip the pieces of steak in the starter mixture, then coat with the flour mixture.

In a large, heavy skillet, heat the lard to 365° F.

(If you don't have a deep-fat frying thermometer, drop in a 1-inch cube of bread. If the bread turns golden brown in 60 seconds, the temperature is right for frying.) Fry the steaks for 8 to 12 minutes, turning carefully with tongs after 5 minutes, until the crust is deep golden brown and the meat is cooked to the desired doneness. Serve hot.

Makes 6 to 8 servings

Scalloped Cabbage

Because it keeps well, cabbage was one of the few fresh vegetables available to chuck-wagon cooks. The recipe that follows is a typical one from the open range days.

¼ cup plus 1 tablespoon butter

2 tablespoons unbleached flour

2 cups milk

Salt and freshly ground pepper

Freshly grated nutmeg, optional

1 medium head cabbage, coarsely chopped

1 cup coarse cracker crumbs, reserve 2 to 3 tablespoons for topping

In saucepan over low heat, melt $^1/_4$ cup butter. Add flour and cook stirring for 3 to 4 minutes, until mixture begins to turn golden. Slowly add milk, stirring constantly. Continue to cook until sauce has thickened. Season to taste with salt and pepper and add a sprinkling of nutmeg if desired.

Preheat oven to 325° F. To a pot of rapidly boiling, lightly salted water add cabbage and cook, covered, until just tender, 8 to 10 minutes. Remove from heat and drain well. Butter a 9-inch square baking pan. Alternate layers of cabbage and crumbs ending with a layer of cabbage. Pour white sauce over cabbage mixture and sprinkle with reserved crumbs. Dot with reserved butter. Bake, uncovered, for about 30 minutes, until the topping is golden brown and the sauce is bubbling.

Serves 4 to 6

King Ranch Beans

In Northern Mexico and Texas, beans are often prepared "ranchero style," with bacon, onions, chiles, and tomatoes. The recipe below is for *Frijoles Rancheros* as they are served at the King Ranch in Texas. (For more information about the King Ranch, see page 112.)

2 cups dried pinto beans

2 cloves garlic, peeled and mashed

1 cup diced bacon

½ cup chopped onion

1 to 2 hot yellow chiles, or 1 to 2 jalapeños, roasted, peeled, and chopped

4 to 5 ripe plum tomatoes, peeled and chopped

1½ to 2 tablespoons chile powder

Salt and ground pepper, to taste

Pick over the beans and rinse under cold running water until the water remains clear. Place the beans in a 3-quart container and add enough soft water or distilled water to cover the beans by about 5 inches. Allow the beans to soak overnight.

Drain the soaked beans and place in a large, heavy nonreactive pot with a lid. Add 8 cups of water and the garlic. Place the pot over medium-high heat and bring to a boil, then reduce the heat to a steady simmer. Check and gently stir the beans every 20 minutes or so, to make sure there is adequate water, at least 1½ to 2 inches above the beans. (If you need to add more water, add boiling water, because cold water tends to toughen the beans.) Cook for 1½ to 2 hours, until the beans are tender. At altitudes of 5,000 feet and above, allow 1–2 hours additional cooking time.

While the beans are cooking, cook the bacon in a large skillet over medium-low heat. Remove it with a slotted spoon and set aside. Add the onion, chiles, and tomatoes to the bacon drippings in the skillet and sauté over medium-high heat for 1–2 minutes, until slightly softened.

When the beans are tender, stir in the bacon, onion mixture, and chili powder. Season to taste with salt and pepper, then simmer for 20–30 minutes to blend the flavors.

Serves 6

OPPOSITE: *King Ranch Beans and Cowboy Frying Pan Bread*

Cold Biscuit Pudding

Great food and good times are always found around the Brooks Ranch chuck wagon. This early 1900s model wagon has been customized and outfitted with everything necessary to prepare and serve hearty meals for the cowhands who operate this thirty-section cow and calf ranch located south of Sweetwater, in Nolan County, Texas. (A section is one square mile.)

Howard Rogers, head cook and ranch foreman for twenty years, prepares his authentic and tasty meals from foodstuffs carried on the wagon. His friend and neighbor, Roger Lister, assists him with the campsite setup, teardown, and meal preparation. When they aren't cooking for the cowboys at the ranch, this team enjoys competing in chuck-wagon cook-offs, and they occasionally cater special events. Their desire to maintain authenticity has won them recognition throughout the great state of Texas as well as in New Mexico and Oklahoma. This is their recipe for an old-time cowboy dessert. Howard likes to serve Cold Biscuit Pudding warm, topped with a generous slathering of his special Whiskey Sauce.

4 eggs, lightly beaten

1 cup sugar

1 cup fresh or reconstituted evaporated milk

1 teaspoon vanilla extract

4 cold biscuits, crumbled

2 tablespoons melted butter

½ cup chopped pecans

½ cup raisins

3 tablespoons flour

¼ teaspoon grated nutmeg

Howard Rogers' Whiskey Sauce (see page 104)

Preheat the oven to 375° F.

In a mixing bowl, combine the eggs, sugar, milk, and vanilla extract. Stir in the crumbled biscuits and melted butter. Toss the pecans and raisins with enough flour to coat them lightly and gently stir them into the pudding mixture. Pour the mixture into a buttered 9-inch pie plate. Sprinkle lightly with nutmeg.

Bake 25 to 30 minutes, until golden brown. Cut the pudding into wedges and serve warm or at room temperature, topped with the Whiskey Sauce.

Serves 4 to 6

Ketcham Canyon Stew

In 1870, a fierce blizzard caused my great-grandfather's cattle to drift away from his Wind Mill Ranch near Cheyenne, Wyoming. The cattle were found in a sheltered canyon nearly twenty miles south, in the Chalk Bluffs of northeastern Colorado. Benjamin Franklin Ketcham took this as a sign and staked his claim in what is now known as Ketcham Canyon.

Men did the cooking on trail drives and roundups. My father's uncles Will and Herb Ketcham—old-style open range cowboys—were used to "doing for themselves." Uncle Herb could whip up a batch of biscuits in a flash and cook most anything in his old Dutch oven. Bacon or coffee left from breakfast became part of a hearty stew served to ravenous cowboys at the noontime dinner. Serve this stew with hot biscuits.

8 strips thick-sliced bacon, chopped

⅓ cup unbleached all-purpose flour

Salt and ½ teaspoon ground black pepper

1 teaspoon dried thyme or sage leaves (optional)

2½ pounds beef chuck or bottom round, cut into 1½-inch cubes

¾ cup chopped onion

1½ cups strong coffee

3 tablespoons chili sauce or ketchup

2 tablespoons molasses

2 tablespoons Worcestershire sauce

18 small boiling onions, peeled

6 small red potatoes, peeled and quartered

4 carrots, peeled, cut into 1½-inch lengths

Chopped fresh parsley for garnish (optional)

In a Dutch oven over medium-low heat, cook the bacon slowly to render the fat. Remove the cooked bacon with a slotted spoon and set aside. Combine the flour, 1 teaspoon of salt, the pepper, and thyme. Pat the beef cubes dry and toss with the flour mixture. Over medium-high heat, brown the beef in the bacon drippings, working in batches if necessary. Remove the browned meat and set it aside. Add the chopped onion to the pan and cook 1 to 2 minutes. Stir in the coffee, chili sauce, molasses, Worcestershire, and reserved beef and bacon. Cover and simmer over low heat for 1 hour, stirring occasionally.

Add the boiling onions and 3 cups of water. Simmer, covered, for 30 minutes. Stir in the potatoes, carrots, and more water, if necessary. Continue to simmer the stew, partially covered, for about 30 minutes, or until the potatoes and carrots are tender. Add salt to taste and serve garnished with fresh parsley, if desired.

Makes 6 servings

PAGES 92–93: *Ketcham Canyon Stew with Grandmother's Baking Powder Biscuits*

Line Camp Rabbit with Gravy

Cowboying was seasonal work for many. After the fall roundup, most ranches cut their labor force, keeping on a few hands at headquarters to do chores and sending out others, usually in pairs, to man the line camps. From these camps, spaced several miles apart, cowboys kept track of the herd over the winter. Line-camp work was lonely and rugged. In the High Plains of Wyoming and Colorado, most line shacks were small and primitive. In more temperate climates, the men sometimes lived in tents.

On larger spreads, a wagon was sent out periodically with supplies, but the men at line camps usually supplemented their diet by hunting. Antelope, deer, and rabbits were a welcome addition to their larders. As a young man, my father's uncle Will Ketcham spent many lonely winters in a small cabin in the Chalk Bluffs of northeastern Colorado. This is his recipe for fried rabbit and gravy.

¼ cup cider vinegar

Salt

1 wild or domestic rabbit, cleaned and cut into serving pieces

½ cup unbleached all-purpose flour

½ cup bacon drippings or vegetable oil

1 (12-ounce) can evaporated milk

Ground black pepper

Cayenne pepper (optional)

In a nonreactive bowl, combine 1 cup of water, the vinegar, and 1 tablespoon of salt. Add the rabbit. If using a wild rabbit, cover and marinate in the refrigerator overnight. With a domestic rabbit, the marinating time may be reduced to as little as 1 hour—or even eliminated. Rinse the rabbit well under cold running water and pat dry with paper towels. Roll the pieces in the flour, reserving 3 tablespoons of the remaining flour for the gravy.

In a large skillet or Dutch oven over medium-high heat, heat the bacon drippings. Add the rabbit pieces and brown on all sides. If necessary, brown the pieces in batches to avoid crowding the pan. Pour off all but about ¹/₄ cup of the drippings from the skillet.

Return all the rabbit pieces to the pan. Cover and reduce the heat to medium-low. Cook, turning occasionally, for 30 minutes. Remove the cover and continue to cook gently for an additional 15 to 20 minutes, until the rabbit is tender and cooked through. Remove the rabbit to a warm serving platter.

Add the reserved flour to the pan drippings. Cook, stirring, for 1 minute. Gradually add the milk and ¹/₄ cup of water. Cook, stirring, until the gravy is smooth and thickened. If it seems too thick, add a little more water. Season the gravy to taste with salt, pepper, and cayenne.

Serves 2 to 4

Way Station Pot Roast and Dumplings

In the late 1850s and 1860s, before the railroads opened up the West, most travelers and the mail were transported by stage coach. By 1860, Concord stages could accommodate up to nine passengers and offered service all the way to California. They averaged five to six miles per hour. Coach travel was a slow, rough, dusty, and often hazardous experience and passengers were usually overjoyed to arrive at a way station, where they could rest and get something to eat before continuing the journey. The quality of the food and accommodations at these stage-coach stops varied, but it was more often bad than good. The famous British explorer Sir Richard Burton made the trip in 1860 and wrote at length about the disgusting food he encountered. Of breakfast at a way station near the current Nebraska-Wyoming border he wrote:

> Our breakfast was prepared in the usual prairie style. First the coffee—three parts burnt beans—which had been duly ground to a fine powder and exposed to the air, lest the aroma should prove too strong for us, was placed on the stove to simmer till every noxious principle was duly extracted from it. Then the rusty bacon cut into thick slices was thrown into the fry-pan; here the gridiron is unknown, and if known would be little appreciated, because it wastes the "drippings," which form with the staff of life a luxurious sop. Thirdly, antelope steak, cut off a corpse suspended for the benefit of flies outside, was placed to stew within influence of the bacon's aroma. Lastly came the bread, which of course should have been "cooked" first. The meal is kneaded with water and a pinch of salt: the raising is done by means of a little sour milk, or more generally the deleterious yeast-powders of the trade. The carbonic acid gas evolved by the addition of water must be corrected and the dough must be expanded by saleratus or prepared carbonate of soda or alkali, and other vile stuff, which communicates to the food the green-yellow tinge, and suggests many of the properties of poison....

The food at the way station near Scottsbluff, Nebraska, was a happy surprise for travelers. This recipe for pot roast with dumplings—made with buffalo or beef—was a standard dish on their menu.

POT ROAST

3 to 4 pound beef pot roast (chuck or rump)

Salt

Unbleached all-purpose flour

¼ cup butter

2 garlic cloves, peeled and crushed

1 large yellow onion, peeled and thinly sliced

1 teaspoon sugar

12 whole peppercorns

12 whole allspice

1 whole bay leaf

1 tablespoon grated fresh horseradish (prepared horseradish will do)

½ cup dry red wine or rum

3 cups small whole carrots

DUMPLINGS

2 cups unbleached all-purpose flour

4 teaspoons baking powder

½ teaspoon salt

1 cup milk

1 tablespoon chopped fresh parsley

1 tablespoon snipped fresh chives

Ground black pepper

Preheat the oven to 325° F.

To make the pot roast, rub the meat with salt and flour. Heat the butter in a large Dutch oven over medium heat. Add the garlic and sauté for 1 to 2 minutes, until golden. Remove the garlic and add the meat. Brown the roast on all sides, 10 to 15 minutes. Remove the roast. Add the onion, sprinkle with the sugar, and cook for 5 to 6 minutes to caramelize. Return the meat to the pan, placing it on top of the onions. Add the peppercorns, allspice, bay leaf, and horseradish. Pour the wine and ¹/₂ cup of water over the roast. (For ample gravy more water may be needed. Add it as necessary during cooking.) Cover and place the roast in the oven for 3 to 4 hours or simmer it on top of the stove over very low heat, until tender. Add the carrots during the last half hour of cooking. Remove the roast to a large warmed platter. Arrange the carrots around the roast and keep warm.

To make the dumplings, combine the flour, baking powder, and salt in a mixing bowl. Stir in the milk, parsley, and chives. If the mixture is too dry, add a little more milk.

Add more water to the pan drippings, if needed to provide enough gravy. Bring to a boil over medium-high heat. Drop the dumpling dough by tablespoonful into the simmering gravy. Cook the dumplings for 6 minutes, uncovered. Cover, reduce heat to medium-low, and cook for an additional 6 minutes.

Place the dumplings around the roast. Stir the gravy until smooth and season to taste with salt and pepper. Pour the gravy into a sauce boat. Slice the roast and serve.

Serves 6 to 8

Fried Apricot Pies

Sue Cunningham and Jean Cates have chuck-wagon cooking in their blood. Their father, Dick Shepherd, cooked for the Matador Land and Cattle Company, one of the largest and most famous ranches in Texas. The sisters grew up watching their father feed hungry cowboys. Sue, Jean, and their brother Clyde have continued the family tradition. Their chuck-wagon cooking team, which also includes Sue's husband Ken, daughter Peggy, and family friend Paul Asky, has won many competitions. In 1994 they were awarded first prize in the World's Richest Chuck-Wagon Cook-Off in Riudoso, New Mexico. Sue and Jean's cookbook, *Chuck Wagon Recipes and Others*, receives high praise from their fellow chuck-wagon cooks (see Mail Order Sources). The sisters are famous for their fried pies. The recipe below is adapted from the one they use in competition.

APRICOT FILLING

1 pound dried apricots

1¼ to 1½ cups sugar, depending on the
  sweetness of the fruit

½ teaspoon grated nutmeg

Dash of salt

¼ cup butter

2 teaspoons lemon juice

3 tablespoons cornstarch (optional)

CRUST FOR FRIED PIES

3 cups unbleached all-purpose flour

1 teaspoon salt

⅔ cup chilled vegetable shortening (see Note)

⅓ cup chilled butter (see Note)

1 egg

Vegetable shortening, for frying

To make the filling, in a saucepan, soak the apricots overnight in enough warm water to cover. Place the saucepan over medium-high heat and bring to a boil. Reduce the heat to low and simmer the apricots, uncovered, for 30 minutes. Stir occasionally, mashing the fruit with a wooden spoon. Add the sugar to taste, the nutmeg, salt, butter and lemon juice. If the mixture seems thin, combine the cornstarch with 2 tablespoons cold water and stir into the apricots. Continue to cook 2 to 3 minutes, until the mixture thickens. Allow to cool while preparing the dough for the pies.

To make the crust, combine the flour and salt in a mixing bowl. Using a pastry blender, cut in the shortening and butter until the mixture resembles coarse crumbs.

Lightly beat the egg in a measuring cup. Add enough cold water to make ³/₄ cup of liquid. Make a well in the flour mixture and add the egg mixture. Stir with a fork until the dough comes together. Gather the dough into a ball. Wrap in plastic wrap and chill for at least 30 minutes.

Divide the dough into balls about 2 inches in diameter. Roll out each ball between sheets of

waxed paper into a 5-inch circle (the size of a 3 pound shortening can lid). Spoon 1 to 2 tablespoons of the filling onto half of each circle, leaving a 1-inch border at the edge. Moisten the edges of the pastry with water. Fold the dough over the filling to form a turnover and press the moistened edges together. Using the tines of a fork dipped in flour, crimp the edges of the pies to seal. Chill the pies while heating the shortening.

In a heavy cast-iron skillet, melt enough shortening to be 1 1/2 inches in depth or use a deep fryer. Heat the shortening to 375° F. Add the pies in batches and fry for 2 minutes on each side, until golden brown. (If you don't have a deep-frying thermometer, see the tip on page 86.) Remove the fried pies with a slotted spoon. Drain on a bed of crumpled paper towels. Cover with additional paper towels and a clean dish cloth to keep pies warm and keep them from collecting moisture.

Makes 18 to 20 pies

NOTE: One cup chilled butter-flavored vegetable shortening can be substituted for the shortening and butter in the crust. Any left over filling may be frozen for future pie making. It is also delicious when spread on hot buttered biscuits.

Dried Apple Pie

Dried apples and prunes were common on the frontier. They were the closest thing to fresh fruit for most cowboys. A good chuck-wagon cook could turn out tasty pies and cobblers using dried fruit, but a popular ditty of the era indicates that some efforts were more successful than others!

Spit in my ear
And tell me lies,
But give me no
Dried apple pies.

2 cups dried apples
1 tablespoon cider vinegar (optional)
1/2 cup sugar
1 teaspoon ground allspice
1 teaspoon ground cinnamon
Dough for a double-crust 8-inch pie crust
3 tablespoons butter

Soak the apples in hot water to cover, mixed with the vinegar, overnight. Drain off the water and mix the apples with the sugar, allspice, and cinnamon.

Preheat the oven to 350° F.

Roll out half of the dough and line an 8-inch pie pan with the bottom crust. Add the apple mixture and dot with the butter. Roll out the top crust. Cover the apples with the crust and seal the edges. Make a few slashes in the top crust for ventilation and bake the pie for about 1 hour, until the crust is golden brown.

Serves 4 to 6

Dried Peach Cobbler with Sourdough Crust

Old-time chuck-wagon cooks had one thing in common: almost all of them were men. Today, women such as Sue Cunningham, Jean Cates, Stella Hughes, and Cathi Gillette have joined the ranks of "pot rastlers" in chuck-wagon cook-offs. The recipe below is adapted from one used in competition by Sue and Jean (who are sisters). Dried fruit cobblers, a favorite cowboy dessert, were easier for a camp cook to prepare than double-crusted pies. The addition of sourdough starter to the crust gives this prize-winning dessert wonderful flavor and texture.

PEACH FILLING

3 (7-ounce) packages dried peaches

1½ to 2 cups sugar, depending on the sweetness of the fruit

½ cup butter

1 tablespoon lemon juice

2 teaspoons ground cinnamon

¾ teaspoon almond extract

Dash of salt

SOURDOUGH CRUST

3 cups unbleached all-purpose flour

2 tablespoons sugar

1 teaspoon salt

1 teaspoon ground cinnamon

½ teaspoon baking powder

1¼ cups chilled vegetable shortening

¾ cup Sourdough Starter (see page 67)

To make the filling, place the peaches in a saucepan with enough warm water to cover. Set the pan aside and allow the peaches to soak for at least 2 hours, until softened. Place the pan over medium-high heat and bring the soaking liquid to a boil. Reduce the heat to low and simmer the peaches for 30 minutes, until very tender. Stir in the sugar to taste, the butter, lemon juice, cinnamon, almond extract, and salt. Pour the peaches into an 8-by-12-inch baking dish and set aside while preparing the crust.

Preheat the oven to 375° F.

To make the crust, place the flour, sugar, salt, cinnamon, and baking powder in a large, nonreactive mixing bowl and mix well. Using a pastry blender or your fingers, cut the shortening into the flour mixture until it resembles coarse crumbs. Make a well in the flour mixture and add the sourdough starter. Stir with a fork until the dough comes together. Gather the dough into a ball.

On a lightly floured surface, roll out the dough to a thickness of about ¹/₄ inch. Use a small biscuit cutter (Sue uses a soup can) to cut out the biscuits. Arrange the biscuits on top of the peaches and bake for 35 to 40 minutes, until the peaches are bubbling and the crust is golden brown.

To cook a cobbler over hot coals, soak and cook the fruit filling in a shallow 12-inch Dutch oven. Top with the biscuits. Preheat the lid of the Dutch oven in the fire. Suspend the Dutch oven over the coals. Carefully lift the oven lid from the fire with a pot hook and tap it against a shovel to jar off any clinging ash. Place the lid on the Dutch oven and use tongs to cover it with an even layer of hot coals. Cook until the peaches are bubbling and the crust is golden brown, checking frequently after 20 minutes.

Serves 10 to 12

Son-of-a-Gun-in-a-Sack

With limited supplies, chuck-wagon cooks had to be creative to provide satisfying desserts for the cowboys. Cowboys craved sweets; this may be related to the fact that in most outfits, alcohol was not allowed on trail drives. A cook who could whip up a tasty cobbler or pudding won high marks with the crew, even if he was ornery and cantankerous. Chuck-wagon staples usually included flour, molasses, dried fruit, salt, and saleratus (baking soda). A well-stocked wagon might also carry some sugar, a few eggs stored between layers of salt, canned evaporated milk, and a closely hoarded stock of seasonings and luxuries such as vanilla and lemon extracts, cinnamon, cloves, nutmeg, and nuts.

The pudding known as Son-of-a-Gun-in-a-Sack was a very special treat. Despite its colorful name, this dessert is really just the cowboy version of English and colonial suet puddings. On the trail, the pudding was mixed and placed in an empty cotton flour or sugar sack. The top of the sack was twisted and tied and the pudding was lowered into a big kettle of boiling water to cook. We couldn't wait to try this traditional recipe but didn't expect to enjoy eating it. We were wrong—it is delicious and fun to make. It is wonderful topped with Howard Rogers' Whiskey Sauce (see page 104) and a dollop of whipped cream.

2 cups unbleached all-purpose flour

1½ cups fresh bread crumbs

½ cup firmly packed brown sugar

1 tablespoon baking soda

1 teaspoon salt

1 teaspoon ground cinnamon

¼ teaspoon ground cloves

¼ teaspoon ground nutmeg

1 cup raisins

1 cup ground suet (5 ounces) or vegetable
     shortening

½ cup chopped walnuts or pecans

1 (5⅓-ounce) can evaporated milk (⅔ cup)

½ cup light molasses

Howard Rogers' Whiskey Sauce (optional; see
     page 104)

Sweetened whipped cream (optional)

In a mixing bowl, combine the flour, bread crumbs, sugar, baking soda, salt, cinnamon, cloves, and nutmeg. Fold in the raisins, suet, and nuts. Stir in the milk and molasses; mix well.

Arrange 6 to 8 layers of cheesecloth to form a 16-inch square. Set in a 1-quart mixing bowl and fill with the pudding mixture. Bring up the sides of the cheesecloth and, leaving room for the pudding to expand, tie tightly with string.

Place the "sack" in a colander. Place the colander in a kettle and add enough boiling water to cover the sack. Cover and boil gently for 2 hours. Carefully lift the colander out of the pan and immediately remove the cheesecloth from around the pudding. Place the pudding, rounded side up, on a plate. Let stand 30 minutes before serving. Serve warm or at room temperature topped with Whiskey Sauce and whipped cream.

Serves 10 to 12

Howard Rogers' Whiskey Sauce

1 cup butter

1 cup sugar

½ cup heavy whipping cream

½ cup half-and-half

¼ cup Jack Daniel's Whiskey

Melt the butter in a cast-iron skillet over medium-low heat. Stir in the sugar and cook, stirring, until the sugar dissolves. Gradually stir in the cream and half-and-half and bring the mixture to a boil over medium-high heat. Cook, stirring, over medium heat for 10 to 12 minutes, until the mixture becomes a smooth, medium-thick sauce. Remove from the heat and stir in the whiskey. Serve the warm sauce spooned over Cold Biscuit Pudding (page 90) or Son-of-a-Gun-in-a-Sack (see page 102).

Makes about 2 cups

No-Egg Squaw Cake

Squaw cake, or Poor Man's Cake, is an old-fashioned mountain man and American Indian dessert. It is a moist gingerbread-like affair, leavened with baking soda and made without eggs or butter. The richness and texture in the earliest versions of the recipe came from rendered bear fat.

Squaw cake remained popular with cowboys on the trail drives during the mid to late 1800s. Eggs and butter were still hard to come by, but beef was plentiful. When an animal was slaughtered, chuck-wagon cooks saved and rendered the mild tasting fat from around the kidneys to use in baking. When old dessert recipes call for "lard," they are referring to this rendered kidney fat from pork, beef, or—in a pinch—bear. Leaf lard has a delicate flavor, very different from the strong, often rancid tasting, commercial lard sold in modern supermarkets. Although vegetable shortening may be substituted for the lard in this recipe (and in most others), the taste will not be the same. For really authentic flavor, ask your butcher to order kidney fat from pork or beef and try making your own leaf lard.

1 cup raisins

1 cup Leaf Lard (see below) or vegetable shortening

1½ cups granulated sugar

½ cup molasses or firmly packed brown sugar

4 cups unbleached all-purpose flour

1 teaspoon baking powder

1 teaspoon ground allspice

1 teaspoon ground cloves

1 teaspoon ground nutmeg

1 teaspoon ground cinnamon

½ teaspoon baking soda

½ teaspoon salt

1 cup chopped nuts (optional)

Preheat the oven to 350° F. Grease and flour a 9-inch springform pan.

Place the raisins in a large saucepan with 2 cups of water. Bring to a boil over high heat. Reduce the heat to medium and simmer for 15 minutes. Remove the pan from the heat and stir in the lard, sugar, and molasses until well combined. Allow the mixture to cool.

Combine the flour, baking powder, allspice, cloves, nutmeg, cinnamon, baking soda, and salt. Stir into the raisin mixture along with the nuts. Pour into the prepared pan. Bake 1 to 1¼ hours, or until a toothpick or clean broom straw inserted in the center of the cake comes out clean.

Serves 8 to 12

Leaf Lard

1 pound kidney fat, from pork or beef

Chop the fat into small pieces and place it in the top of a double boiler over boiling water. Cook gently for about 1 hour, until the fat is melted.

Line a large strainer with cheesecloth. Pour the hot fat through the strainer into a small crock. Chill until hardened, then cover tightly and store for up to one month in the refrigerator or indefinitely in the freezer.

Makes 2 cups

THE BIG RANCHES

*F*OR MANY NORTH AMERICANS, the large and sprawling cattle ranches scattered across the western United States and Canada are symbols of the romance often associated with the Old West. They are still wide open spaces, promising freedom and a simpler life. Like the cowboy, such ranches first appeared in New Spain—which included Spanish Texas and California.

Of course, ranching continued after Texas and California became part of the United States, but in California it began to decline in the 1850s, following the discovery of gold and the rush of forty-niners settling there. In Texas, however, cattle ranching continued to prosper, and huge ranches were established on lands too dry to farm.

The first man to control a huge ranch in the United States was John Chisum, who took up ranching in north Texas in 1857. When settlers began crowding him, he moved near where San Angelo, Texas, now stands. In 1866, after the government contracted with him to deliver cattle to feed soldiers and Indians in New Mexico, Chisum controlled a vast region covering southeastern New Mexico and portions of west Texas. He set up his ranch headquarters at Bosque Grande, thirty miles south of Fort Sumner, New Mexico. His range embraced far more than a million acres, a vast area two hundred miles long and thirty miles wide, with upwards of one hundred thousand cattle and more than one hundred cowboys.

Chisum's El Rancho Grande house was always open to visitors, and his dining table was ready—seven days a week—to seat forty guests at a moment's notice. The food that was served there included American, Mexican, and Indian dishes. In 1879, when cattlemen from Texas challenged Chisum for land he did not own, he sold what property he did own and moved to Santa Fe. He died there in 1884.

One rancher who did own his huge ranch was Lucian Maxwell, who came west in 1840 to trap and trade furs. After his marriage in 1844, Maxwell acquired an interest in the huge Beautiben-Miranda land grant east of Taos, New Mexico. Buying up other interests in the grant, Maxwell soon owned some 97,000 acres, extending from near modern Springer, New Mexico, north into Colorado.

Maxwell built a large mansion with forty rooms at Cimarron, New Mexico, and made it his ranch headquarters. His hospitality was well known, both in his "council hall" and around his dining table, where he entertained such illustrious westerners as Kit Carson. He sold out to a group of capitalists in 1870 and died in Santa Fe five years later.

Another large ranch was started in 1853 by Richard King, who had been a steamboat captain on the lower Rio Grande. By the late 1860s he had acquired some 84,000 acres along the Gulf Coast of south Texas. Before 1900, his ranch had grown to 1,270,000 acres—the largest parcel of land under one owner anywhere in the world at the time. At one point, the King Ranch had more than one hundred and twenty-five thousand cattle and thousands of horses. Some three hundred cowboys or *vaqueros* worked on the ranch. The King Ranch continues to operate today.

After the Indians on the northern plains were placed on reservations, following General George Armstrong Custer's defeat at the Battle of the Little Big Horn in 1876, cattle ranching spread onto the northern plains. Large ranches were established in Colorado, Wyoming, Montana, Dakota Territory, and Nebraska. While none of them reached the size of the King Ranch in Texas, they were still extremely large, comprising thousands of acres.

But when barbed wire was introduced, cattlemen began to fence their ranches with "the devil's hatband," as it was sometimes called. Barbed wire told outsiders not to trespass and it enabled ranchers to control their cattle and begin livestock breeding programs. Barbed wire also changed ranching practices. Cowboys spent many more nights sleeping in the bunkhouse, and a cook prepared breakfast before the cowboys would ride out to perform their daily chores, which might include riding the fence line and repairing any broken barbed wire or treating sick or injured cattle. At night, supper was served.

Twice yearly, the cowboys would round up cattle on the ranch and brand the new calves. They gathered up the steers going to market and drove them to the nearest railroad station for shipment. Each large ranch operated its own chuck wagon, with a cook to feed the cowboys during round-ups. Coffee and meat—beef, bacon, salt pork, or wild game—continued as the mainstay of the cowboy's diet. Dried or canned products including beans, rice, hominy, raisins, onions, apples, potatoes, and pickles, supplemented with wild fruit in season and bread, cornbread, or biscuits, usually filled out the menu.

When fresh vegetables and fruit were served, they disappeared rapidly. After canned goods became available in the late 1870s, the cowboy's diet improved. Canned vegetables such as corn and peas were not particularly popular, but canned tomatoes—with their tangy acidity—were craved. Tomatoes were also a good thirst quencher, and tomatoes stewed with a little sugar were a favorite accompaniment of biscuits for many cowboys.

Some old-time cowboys claimed that the food served by many ranches on the northern plains was far better than that served by ranchers on the southern plains. A wider selection of food products may have been responsible in part, but by the early 1880s many northern ranches were owned by large eastern or foreign syndicates, which sought to attract cowboys from the southern plains to come work for them in the north and spared no expense in doing so.

Many of the large ranches of the nineteenth century contributed to the cuisine of ranch country, a cuisine found today not only at the dining tables on many western ranches but in countless other places throughout the United States and Canada. —DAVID DARY

PIERCE RANCH AND RUNNELLS-PIERCE RANCH
Texas

Shanghai Pierce was one of the most colorful and dynamic of all Texas cattlemen. He built a cattle empire that at its height spread over a million acres. He is credited with introducing the first Brahman cattle to Texas, which is a story in itself.

Abel Head Pierce, called "Shanghai" because he was tall, redheaded, and reminded folks of a Shanghai rooster, came to Texas in the early 1850s as a nineteen-year-old stowaway. The ship put him ashore at the port of Indianola. From the beginning, Pierce's exploits and adventures were memorable. As a young cowboy, he was hired to drive a herd of Longhorns overland to New Orleans. In his book *Cowboy Culture*, David Dary includes Pierce's account of the journey as told in *Shanghai Pierce: A Fair Likeness* by Chris Emmitt.

> The mud and water of the Louisiana swamps compelled us to pick every step. Why the public roads—where there were any—would bog a saddleblanket. My steers were nice, fat, slick critters that knew how to swim, but they were used to a carpet of prairie grass. They were mighty choosey as to where they put their feet. They had a bushel of sense: and purty soon over there in Louisiana they got to balancing theirselves on logs in order to keep out of the slimy mud. Yes, they got so expert that one of them would walk a cypress knee to the stump, jump over it, land on a root, and walk it out for another jump. If there was a bad bog-hole between cypresses you'd see a steer hang his 'orns into a mustang-grapevine, or maybe a wisteria, and swing across like a monkey. The way they balanced and jumped and swung actually made my horse laugh.

Shanghai knew how to spin a yarn and no one who met him ever forgot him.

Pierce, who referred to himself as "Webster on Cattle," searched for a breed that would be perfectly suited to the hot, humid climate along the Gulf Coast. He settled on the Brahman cattle of India. Unfortunately, Pierce didn't live to see his first Brahmas arrive at the quarantine station in New York. When the authorities wanted to destroy the animals, his nephew A. P. Borden went to the White House to see Teddy Roosevelt. Luckily, President Roosevelt was sympathetic to the plight of a fellow rancher and the Brahmas went to Texas.

We are sure that the addictively delicious pecan cookies made by Leola, the beloved cook at the modern-day Runnells-Pierce Ranch, would have made a hit with those old-time cowboys.

Leola's Pecan Cookies

3 ½ cups sifted unbleached all-purpose flour

½ teaspoon baking soda

1 ½ cups butter, softened

3 cups firmly packed brown sugar

3 large eggs

3 cups chopped toasted pecans

Sift together the flour and the baking soda. Cream the butter in a mixing bowl. Add the sugar and beat until the mixture is fluffy. Add the eggs, one at a time, and beat until well combined. Add the flour mixture and blend. Stir in the pecans. Chill the dough, covered, at least 2 hours.

Preheat the oven to 350° F.

Scoop walnut-size pieces of dough and roll into balls. Place the balls 2 inches apart on a lightly buttered cookie sheet. Flatten each ball slightly with the palm of your hand. Bake the cookies until golden brown, 10 to 12 minutes.

Makes 4 to 5 dozen

NOTE: If desired, use half the dough and store the remaining dough, covered, in the refrigerator. It also freezes well.

See photograph, page 106.

KING RANCH
Texas

The King Ranch, founded in 1853 by Captain Richard King, stretches across 835,000 acres of south Texas. One of the world's largest and most historic ranches, it is a recognized leader in the ranching industry. The majestic, red Santa Gertrudis—the first American cattle breed—was developed here over years of selective cross-breeding of Brahman and Shorthorn cattle.

Richard King was born in New York in 1824 and worked as a young man as a riverboat pilot. King came to Texas during the war with Mexico in 1847. In partnership with a friend named Mifflin Kenedy, he started a riverboat company and began transporting troops and supplies up the Rio Grande. He became acquainted with Robert E. Lee, then assigned to the Department of Texas by the U. S. Army. Lee convinced King that the area between the Nueces and Rio Grande rivers, known as the Wild Horse Desert, had great potential as cattle country.

At the time, the Wild Horse Desert was a wild place indeed. Bands of outlaws and rustlers rode roughshod over those brave or foolish enough to settle there. Undaunted, Richard King established the headquarters for his new ranch on the banks of Santa Gertrudis Creek, the only source of fresh water in the area.

Captain King patterned his ranch on the haciendas and ranchos of northern Mexico. He supplemented the wild cattle already on the range with additional Longhorn stock from ranchos across the border. A cattle ranch needs cowboys, so in 1854 King traveled to Mexico to hire vaqueros. He returned to Texas with the inhabitants of an entire village. The party numbered approximately 120 men, women, and children, along with their livestock and possessions. With the help of these vaquero families, who became known as *Los Kinenos* (the people of King Ranch), Richard King and his wife, Henrietta, built a ranching empire.

The influence of the original founders remains strong at the King Ranch today. The ranch is still owned and operated by descendants of Richard and Henrietta King and most of the ranch staff descends from the original *Kinenos*.

King Ranch cuisine is a combination of northern Mexican, Tex-Mex, Native American, and European cooking styles. Beef is plentiful and both exotic and native wild game are abundant on the ranch. Seafood arrives fresh from the Gulf Coast and the fertile Rio Grande valley supplies vegetables and fruit. Thanks to Janell and Tio Kleberg and several other great King Ranch cooks who have generously shared their recipes, even armchair cowboys can sample the fine food and Texas hospitality for which this ranch is famous.

Tío Kleberg's Hot Sauce

This is a salsa with authority! If you like it mild, use the smaller amount of chiles—or even less. According to the *King Ranch Cookbook* (see Mail-Order Sources), chiles piquin vary in heat according to the weather. Generally, the drier the year, the hotter the chile.

⅓ cup peeled and chopped onion

2 to 4 tablespoons of chile piquin, fresh off the bush,

or 1 to 1½ fresh jalapeños, seeded

1 tablespoon vinegar

1 tablespoon olive oil

1 (10-ounce) can Rotel tomatoes or Mexican- or Spanish-style

tomatoes with green chiles

Salt

Place the onion, chiles, ¼ cup of water, the vinegar, and oil in a food processor fitted with the steel blade or a blender. Process to the texture you prefer, chunky or pureed. Add the tomatoes and process briefly. Season with salt to taste.

Makes about 1¾ cups

Roasted Pepper and Tomato Relish

Johnny Gonzales is a unit manager on the Norias division of the King Ranch. Working with cattle is his first love, but he enjoys cooking on weekends. We think his steak with roasted pepper and tomato relish is outstanding.

2 bell peppers (1 red and 1 yellow)

1 medium tomato, diced

1 medium green tomato, diced

1 small red onion, peeled and chopped

2 tablespoons olive oil

1 tablespoon red wine vinegar

2 tablespoons minced fresh cilantro

¼ teaspoon salt

Preheat the oven to 450° F.

Prick the bell peppers in several places with a fork. Place on a baking sheet or in a shallow roasting pan. Roast the peppers for 30 minutes, or until the skin is blackened. Transfer the peppers to a paper bag, close the bag, and allow the peppers to steam for about 10 minutes.

Meanwhile, combine the tomatoes and onion in a nonreactive bowl. Stir in the oil, vinegar, cilantro, and salt. Remove the peppers from the bag and peel off the skin. Seed and dice the peppers and stir into the tomato mixture. Cover and refrigerate for at least 1 hour before serving.

Makes about 3 cups

King Ranch Chili Steaks

1 teaspoon coarsely ground black pepper

4 T-Bone or rib eye steaks (8–10 ounces each)

⅓ cup fresh lime juice

3 tablespoons olive oil

1 tablespoon chili powder

¼ teaspoon dried Mexican oregano leaves (see Mail-Order Sources) or regular oregano

Roasted Pepper and Tomato Relish (see page 113)

Lime wedges and fresh cilantro sprigs, for garnish

Press pepper onto both sides of each steak, using $^1/_4$ teaspoon pepper for each steak. In a shallow nonreactive baking dish, combine the lime juice, olive oil, chili powder, and oregano. Place the steaks in the lime mixture. Cover and marinate, refrigerated, for 4 hours, turning occasionally. Remove the steaks from the marinade and grill or broil 3 to 4 minutes on each side for medium-rare to medium. Spoon the relish over the steaks. Garnish with lime wedges and cilantro sprigs.

Makes 4 to 6 servings

King Ranch Chili Steak with Roasted Pepper and Tomato Relish

THE FOUR SIXES
Texas

The four Burnett Ranches have become known as the Four Sixes, referring to the brand "6666" that Burnett cattle have worn for more than a century. Legend has it that Captain Samuel "Burk" Burnett won the original ranch in a poker game with a winning hand of four sixes, a story that is colorful but untrue. In fact, when young Burk Burnett purchased his first hundred head of cattle in 1867, the herd already carried this now-famous brand. He bought the brand, too, and continued to use it as he built his ranch empire.

Samuel Burnett was born on a farm in Bates County, Missouri, in 1849. After their house was destroyed in the bloody Ruffian and Jayhawkers raids of 1857 and 1858, his family headed for Texas. There, on the open range, the Burnetts entered the cattle business.

One of the first casualties of western development was the open range. To remain in the cattle business, the ranch owner had to own his land—and plenty of it. Burk Burnett anticipated this turn of events and set about buying land. During the late 1800s he also arranged to lease grazing rights from the Kiowa and Comanche on their reservation north of the Red River in Oklahoma. He respected the Indians' rights and developed a friendship with Comanche Chief Quanah Parker that lasted through both their lifetimes. Burk Burnett's ranches are now owned and operated by his great granddaughter, Ann Burnett Windfohr Marion, and comprise the largest individually owned ranch property in Texas, some 480,000 acres.

The Four Sixes is known for producing high-quality beef, and the ranch cooks are always adding new beef recipes to their menus. The beef carbonnade recipe that follows is a favorite. Many thanks to Shonda Gibson of the Four Sixes for sharing it with us.

Four Sixes' Beef Carbonnade

3 pounds beef stew meat, cut into 1 inch cubes

½ cup vegetable oil

6 cups thinly sliced onions

3 tablespoons unbleached all-purpose flour

2 cups beer, preferably dark beer

1 cup beef broth

1 tablespoon wine vinegar

1 teaspoon brown sugar

1 clove garlic, peeled and minced

½ teaspoon dried thyme

1 bay leaf

Salt and ground black pepper

½ pound mushrooms, trimmed and sliced

2 tablespoons chopped fresh parsley

Preheat the oven to 325° F.

Pat the beef dry with paper towels. In a large skillet over medium-high heat, heat ¼ cup of the oil. Add the beef and brown it in 2 or 3 batches, adding more oil if necessary. Remove the beef to a heavy casserole with a lid. Add the onions to the skillet and sauté until translucent, 2 to 3 minutes. Remove the onions to the casserole.

Add all but 2 tablespoons of the remaining oil and the flour to the skillet and stir over low heat for about 5 minutes, until the flour turns a nutty brown. Gradually stir in the beer and broth. Cook, stirring and scraping the pan with a wire whisk, until the liquid is slightly thickened. Add the vinegar, sugar, garlic, thyme, bay leaf, and salt and pepper to taste. Bring to a boil and pour over the beef and onions in the casserole. Cover tightly with the lid, place in the oven, and cook for 2 hours, or until the meat is fork-tender. Remove and discard the bay leaf. Just before serving, sauté the mushrooms in the reserved 2 tablespoons of oil for 2 minutes, until lightly browned. Add the mushrooms to the stew. Serve sprinkled with the parsley.

Serves 6 to 8

LASATER RANCH
Texas

La Mota, the headquarters of the Lasater Ranch, is located near the town of Falfurrias in south Texas. A grove of ancient live oaks surrounds La Mota, making it an oasis in the sunbaked prairie. The ranch was founded in 1893 by Edward C. Lasater, a cattleman who, during a terrible drought, saw the potential in this country. Before 1910, his ranch was larger than the state of Rhode Island.

In a quest to find the ideal breed of cattle for his arid land, Ed Lasater introduced Brahman cattle to south Texas in 1908. He also developed a superior herd of Hereford cattle with distinctive red circles around the eyes, which protected them from the glare of the fierce Texas sun and made them resistant to the eye troubles that often afflict white-faced cattle.

A portion of the ranch was also devoted to a dairy operation. Mr. Lasater imported a herd of purebred Jersey cows from England and started a creamery at Falfurrias that became famous for its butter. The Falfurrias Creamery Company was the centerpiece of Ed Lasater's dream of developing a diversified agricultural community. Toward that dream, he sold a large portion of his ranch in pieces to farmers and dairymen.

Lasater's ranch was greatly diminished during the 1920s and much of the land had to be sold during the depression. After Edward Lasater's death in 1930, his sons Garland and Tom returned to manage the ranch and creamery.

Tom Lasater continued his father's program of crossbreeding the ranch herds of Brahman and Hereford cattle with Shorthorns. In the 1940s, Tom moved to Matheson, Colorado, to start his own ranch. He continued his breeding program and in 1954 the USDA recognized his Beefmaster cattle as a distinct American breed.

Garland Lasater remained in Falfurrias to carry on the creamery and dairy operations. The La Mota headquarters and some of the most beautiful portions of the ranch are still owned by the Lasater family today. Garland's children, grandchildren, and great-grandchildren return each Thanksgiving. After a day spent hunting, the Lasaters and their friends gather around a hot mesquite or oak campfire to feast on venison backstrap sautéed with lots of Falfurrias butter in a huge, old, black-iron skillet. The backstrap is the tenderloin of venison. It is lean and delicate and should not be overcooked. Garland Lasater knows how to cook venison and we are delighted to include his recipe in this book.

OPPOSITE: *Garland Lasater's Sautéed Venison Backstrap*

Garland Lasater's Sautéed Venison Backstrap

2 to 2½ pound venison backstrap (tenderloin),
trimmed with membrane removed, thinly sliced
¼ cup fresh lime juice
2 garlic cloves, peeled and crushed
Salt and freshly ground black pepper
6–8 tablespoons good-quality butter, such as Falfurrias butter

Place the venison slices in a shallow nonreactive baking dish and coat with the lime juice, garlic, and salt and pepper to taste. Allow to marinate in a refrigerator or cooler for about 1 hour. Remove the slices and place them on a jelly-roll pan lined with paper towels. Top with more paper towels to absorb the excess marinade.

Melt 3 tablespoons of the butter in a very large, heavy cast-iron skillet over red-hot embers from a campfire or over medium-high heat on the stove top. As soon as the butter begins to turn clear, place as many slices in the pan as will fit without touching. Sauté them quickly, 1 to 2 minutes per side, until lightly browned on the outside and red to pink inside. Remove the fillets to a warm platter. Repeat with the remaining butter and venison, until all the slices are cooked. Serve with warm flour or corn tortillas and either Salsa Mexicana (see page 51) or Tio Kleberg's Hot Sauce (see page 113).

Serves 6 to 8

NOTE: If your skillet is not large enough to sauté the venison without crowding, two skillets can be used at the same time, or divide the butter and cook the venison in batches.

WARREN LIVESTOCK
Wyoming

In the 1870s, despite the fact that "cattle was king," one of the largest ranching operations in the West was built largely on sheep. Francis E. Warren, the founder of Warren Livestock and a prominent figure in Wyoming history, was one of the first ranchers in the high plains to graze both sheep and cattle on the same range. This was an unusual idea at a time when cattlemen and sheepmen were often violently at odds, but Warren was not easily intimidated. In 1894, Warren Livestock was running 63,433 sheep, 3,220 cattle, 1,826 horses, and 26 mules on a huge tract of land that stretched from Laramie, Wyoming, to Fort Collins, Colorado, and east to the border of Nebraska.

Francis Warren's ranching venture was a success and so was his political career. He served as mayor of Cheyenne, was appointed governor of Wyoming Territory by President Chester A. Arthur, and was later elected governor of the newly chartered state. In 1890 he was elected to the United States Senate, and he was regularly re-elected until his death in 1929.

While the Senator was in Washington, the management of the vast holdings of Warren Livestock was taken over by his son Frederick F. Warren, and later by his grandson Francis E. Warren, III. In 1963 the current owner, Paul Etchepere, bought the company with a group of investors.

In 1890, while Senator Warren was building his empire, a young Basque immigrant named John Etchepere arrived in California to work as a sheepherder. John Etchepere prospered, and today his descendants own and operate one of the most successful and progressive sheep and cattle operations in the West.

Good food is a tradition at Warren Livestock. At the Pole Creek Ranch, Olaya Izaguirre cooks for an international crew of herders from Spain, Mexico, and Chile. Olaya was born in Spain and prepares many great Spanish dishes, but she is known especially for her delicious pies. She uses an old-fashioned American pie crust that includes vinegar and produces crusts that are wonderfully tender and flaky. We are lucky to include her recipe for Cherry Pie.

Helen Etchepere is also a wonderful cook. She has been kind enough to share with us an old Basque family recipe for lamb stew.

Basque Lamb Stew

3 pounds boneless lamb shoulder, trimmed of
    excess fat
2 tablespoons olive oil
5 tablespoons butter
2 celery stalks, finely chopped
2 carrots, finely chopped
2 medium onions, peeled and finely chopped
4 cloves garlic, peeled and minced
3 tablespoons unbleached all-purpose flour
¾ teaspoon dried thyme

Salt and ground black pepper
2 cups dry red wine
1 bay leaf

VEGETABLES
1 pound potatoes, cut into walnut size pieces
1 pound carrots, cut into walnut size pieces
1 onion, peeled and chopped
1 ½ cups fresh or frozen green peas

Cut the lamb into 1¹/₂ inch cubes. Heat the oil and 3 tablespoons of butter in a deep Dutch oven over medium-high heat. Pat the meat dry and add to the Dutch oven in several batches to avoid crowding the pan. Brown on all sides. Remove the meat from the pan. Add the the remaining 2 tablespoons butter, celery, carrots, onions, and garlic to the pan and sprinkle with the flour. Cook, stirring frequently, for 3 to 4 minutes, until the flour is a nutty brown color. Return the lamb to the pan and pour in the wine and enough hot water to cover the lamb. Add the thyme and bay leaf and season with salt and

pepper. Cover and simmer over low heat for about 1¹/₂ hours, until the lamb is tender. Remove from the heat and refrigerate overnight to allow any fat to solidify.

Skim off the fat from the top of the stew and return the pan to the stove. If the sauce seems too thick, add a little additional wine or water. Add the potatoes, carrots, and onion and cook for 30 minutes. Stir in the peas and cook an additional 10 minutes. Taste and adjust the seasonings. Remove the bay leaf and serve.

Serves 6 to 8

Olaya's Cherry Pie

CRUST

3 cups unbleached all-purpose flour

1 teaspoon salt

1 cup lard or vegetable shortening

1 large egg

1 teaspoon cider vinegar

FILLING

²/₃ to 1 cup sugar, depending on the sweetness of the cherries

3 tablespoons cornstarch

4 cups fresh, frozen, or partially drained canned pie cherries (reserve liquid)

¼ teaspoon almond extract

Red food coloring (optional)

ASSEMBLY

2 tablespoons cream

2 tablespoons sugar

To make the crust, combine the flour and salt in a mixing bowl. Cut in the lard using a pastry blender.

Put the egg and vinegar in a measuring cup and beat while adding enough cold water to make ³/₄ cup liquid. Make a well in the flour and add the liquid. Stir with a fork until the dough comes together. If the dough seems moist, place it in the refrigerator for a while to firm.

Roll one-third of the dough into a round ¹/₈ inch thick and gently press it into a 9-inch pie plate. Roll out another third of the dough and cut into strips to form a lattice top.

To make the filling, combine the sugar and cornstarch in a saucepan. Add ¹/₄ cup of cold water or cherry juice and stir until smooth. Add the cherries.

Cook over medium heat 3 to 4 minutes, until the juices begin to thicken. Add the almond extract and a few drops food coloring, if desired. Remove from the heat and cool.

Preheat the oven to 425° F.

Pour the filling into the unbaked pie shell. Cover the filling with the lattice top, seal, and flute the edges. Brush the top with the cream and sprinkle with the sugar. Place the pie on a baking sheet to avoid spills in the oven. Place the baking sheet on the bottom shelf of the oven and bake for 15 minutes. Reduce the oven temperature to 350° F and continue to bake for 35 to 40 minutes more, until the filling is bubbling and the crust is golden brown.

Serves 4 to 6

RANCHO "EL ALAMO"
Mexico

After General McClellan gave his approval to a strange-looking saddle with a slit down the middle, it was adopted by the United States Army as the official saddle for the Cavalry. The invention of this saddle—thereafter called the McClellan saddle—ensured the fortunes of the Kibbey family of Washington, D.C., who manufactured it.

In 1900, young William Beckford Kibbey III received notice from Harvard College that he had been "rusticated," a polite way of advising a student that he had been kicked out. The family decided that he might as well go to work. Since several of his father's friends had mining interests in Arizona and northern Mexico, "Beck" Kibbey was sent out to work in the mines.

The sophisticated young easterner, fluent in German and French, soon learned Spanish and became a popular figure in Tucson society. Through Ramon Elias, a friend from one of Tucson's old aristocratic Mexican families, Kibbey was given the opportunity to become a partner in a great Spanish land grant in northern Sonora called El Alamo (The Cottonwood). Kibbey and Elias bought out the other partners and stocked the 275,000-acre ranch with 10,000 Longhorn heifers and 500 young bulls.

With the help of his friends and a crew of Mexican vaqueros, William Kibbey built a remarkable adobe citadel on the ranch. This fortified mansion was the site of many wonderful parties and also, on occasion, had to be defended against marauding bandits and revolutionaries.

Beck Kibbey married Josephine Mix and the couple raised their two daughters, Judy and Sallie, on the ranch. The family no longer owns El Alamo but Judy's daughter, Jean Neubauer of Tumacacori, Arizona, has given us this recipe for a special flaming Christmas punch made with mescal that her grandparents served at El Alamo.

Sonoran Christmas Punch

Jean Neubauer reminds us that mescal is a very strong spirit and that proportions can be adapted to suit individual tastes.

3 cups fresh orange juice

1 cup fresh lemon juice

1 cup sugar

3 cups brewed tea

1½ to 3 cups mescal

1 to 2 oranges, thinly sliced

In a large saucepan, dissolve the sugar in the fruit juices over low heat. Stir in the tea and mescal. Pour the punch into a pot that can be set in the fireplace on hot coals. Float the orange slices in the punch. For a festive effect, use a long fireplace match to set the punch aflame just before serving. When the flames begin to die down, ladle the punch into cups and serve.

Makes 12 cups

ILIFF RANCH
Colorado

John Wesley Iliff was the undisputed "cattle king of the plains" in the 1860s and 70s. He came to Colorado in the gold rush of 1859 and started his empire as a trader, buying footsore and exhausted cattle and oxen from wagon trains. Iliff fattened the cattle on the nutritious grasses of the Colorado plains and sold them to the miners. In 1866, after Charles Goodnight and Oliver Loving pioneered their trail from Texas, he bought what remained of their herd. Iliff cattle ranged over thousands of acres from Cheyenne, Wyoming, to Greeley, Colorado, and east to Nebraska.

In 1868, Iliff, who was a widower, met Miss Elizabeth Fraser, a saleswoman for the Singer Sewing Machine Company. He "liked her spunk," and, after a two-year courtship, they were married. Mrs. Iliff was a good cook and an excellent businesswoman. After John Iliff died in 1878, Elizabeth Iliff successfully managed his vast cattle empire. She was known as "the richest woman in Colorado" and was respected for her competence and dignity. Her pie recipe is delicious and unusual for that era. It reminds us of modern recipes for pies and quiches that form their own crust.

Mrs. Iliff's Surprising Pie

1 cup unbleached all-purpose flour

¾ cup sugar

1 teaspoon baking powder

½ teaspoon salt

⅓ cup butter, softened

½ cup milk

½ teaspoon vanilla extract

2 large eggs

1 unbaked 9½- or 10-inch deep-dish pie shell, in a glass pie pan

SAUCE

2 ounces unsweetened chocolate

1 cup sugar

⅓ cup butter

1 teaspoon vanilla extract

½ cup chopped nuts

Whipped cream or vanilla ice cream

Chocolate shavings

Preheat the oven to 350° F.

Sift together the flour, sugar, baking powder, and salt. In a mixing bowl combine the butter, milk, and vanilla. Add the flour mixture and beat for 2 minutes. Add the eggs and beat for 2 minutes longer. Pour the mixture into the unbaked pie shell.

To make the sauce, melt the chocolate in ¾ cup of boiling water in a saucepan. Add the sugar and bring to a boil. Remove from the heat and stir in the butter and vanilla. Pour the chocolate sauce over the pie batter. Sprinkle the nuts over the top.

Bake for 55 to 60 minutes or until set in the middle. Allow the pie to cool. Decorate the top with whipped cream rosettes and chocolate shavings, or serve with ice cream.

Serves 6 to 8

SWAN LAND AND CATTLE CO.
Wyoming

Big ranches are started by bold thinkers. In the 1870s and 80s, one of the boldest ranchers in Wyoming was Alexander Hamilton Swan. Swan, a native of Pennsylvania, came west in 1873 and started a cattle company in partnership with his brothers. The venture failed because of severe winter weather, but Swan persisted and in 1883—backed by more than $3 million in Scottish capital—he started his own firm, the Swan Land and Cattle Co. Swan is credited with introducing the Hereford breed to Wyoming. At one point the company ran more than 100,000 cattle and owned or controlled some 6,000,000 acres from Ogallala, Nebraska, to Fort Steele, Wyoming.

Alexander Swan was a controversial figure in Wyoming history. In his book *My Life on the Range*, John Clay described him as "about six feet and an inch, and wherever he went he made an imposing figure. His face was close shaven, he had a keen eye, a Duke of Wellington nose, and gold teeth. While his manner was casual it was magnetic and he had a great following. At Cheyenne, groups of men sat around him in his office and worshipped at his feet. In Chicago he was courted by bankers, commission men, and breeders of fine cattle; in fact, all classes of people in the livestock business. The mercantile agencies rated him at a million, while I doubt, so far as the range is concerned, if he ever owned an honest dollar."

Whether or not Mr. Clay's assessment of Mr. Swan was correct, Alexander Swan and many other cattlemen on the northern plains were ruined by the terrible blizzards of 1886–87. That winter, Swan's herds were reduced from 113,500 to 57,000 head. In May 1887, Swan Land and Cattle went into receivership and Alexander Swan was asked to resign. His own fortune was lost in bankruptcy proceedings. Swan Land and Cattle continued on a reduced scale under the management of John Clay until its liquidation in 1947.

Swan Land and Cattle was famous for having good food. Mrs. Swan, the former Lizzy Richie of Green County, Pennsylvania, set a fine table at the family's town house in Cheyenne. At the ranches, the culinary skills of Edward Held of the Two Bar and Anna Austin of the TY lured many cowboys to ride for these two famous Swan brands. I found this recipe for Mrs. Swan's white cake in an old Cheyenne cookbook that belonged to my grandmother. The cover is gone, but the names of people who contributed recipes and the advertisements from local merchants indicate that the book was published near the end of the nineteenth century.

Mrs. Swan's White Cake

WHITE CAKE

3 ½ cups unbleached all-purpose flour

1 tablespoon baking powder

¾ cup butter, softened

1 ½ cups sugar

1 cup water

6 egg whites

1 teaspoon vanilla extract

LEMON CURD FILLING

¼ cup butter

¾ cup sugar

2 large eggs

¼ cup fresh lemon juice

1-2 teaspoons finely grated lemon zest

FROSTING

1 cup dried sweetened coconut

¼ cup hot milk

1 large egg white

1 cup sugar

1 cup chopped raisins (optional)

Preheat the oven to 350° F.

To make the cake, lightly grease and flour two 8-inch round cake pans.

Combine the flour and baking powder. In a large mixing bowl, cream the butter and sugar until fluffy, gradually adding ¼ cup of water. Stir in ¾ cup of water. Add the dry ingredients to the batter and blend.

Beat the egg whites until stiff peaks form and fold into the flour mixture. Stir in the vanilla. Pour the batter into the prepared pans and bake for 20 to 25 minutes, until a wooden pick inserted in the center of the cake comes out clean. Cool the cakes on a wire rack. Using a serrated knife, carefully split each layer in half, making a total of 4 layers.

To make the filling, melt the butter in a heavy bottomed saucepan, and add the sugar. Beat in the eggs. Add the lemon juice and lemon zest to taste.

Place the saucepan over medium-low heat. Cook, stirring constantly, until the mixture thickens. Allow the lemon curd to cool, then spread between the layers of the cake.

To make the frosting, soak the coconut in the milk.

Using an electric mixer, beat the egg white in a metal bowl until it forms soft peaks.

In a small saucepan, combine the sugar and ½ cup of water. Bring to a boil and cook until the syrup forms a medium-firm ball when a few drops are dropped in cold water. Slowly pour the boiling syrup into the beaten egg white, beating constantly, until the mixture reaches a spreadable consistency. Squeeze the coconut to remove the milk. Fold the coconut and raisins, if desired, into the frosting. Spread the frosting over the cake.

Serves 8 to 10

OPPOSITE: *Mrs. Swan's White Cake, Texas Apple Cake, and Chocolate Torte Cake*

KENDRICK RANCHES
Wyoming and Montana

John Kendrick's life embodies the American dream. He started life as a penniless orphan and became one of the wealthiest men in the West, the governor of Wyoming, and a United States senator.

John Benjamin Kendrick was born in Cherokee County, Texas, in 1857. At age twenty-two he signed on as a cowboy, helping to bring a Texas herd north to the grasslands of Wyoming. The trip was perilous and he later recalled that:

> Anything at night almost, a stumbling horse, the odor of some wild animal or a blinding flash of lightning would start the herd running. Then the cowboys would have to follow. Sometimes the cattle would run until morning. Or they might stop now and then for a few minutes. Whereupon, of course we would halt with them, the rain meanwhile coming down in torrents and the night being so black that nothing could be seen but the electricity on our horses' ear or the lightning wriggling over the ground like illuminated serpents.

Largely self-educated, Kendrick was a cultivated and intelligent man. He started small, using his cowboy wages to buy a few cattle, which his employer and future father-in-law, Charles Wulfjen, allowed him to graze with the main herd. From those humble beginnings he built up a two-million-acre cattle empire, stretching from northern Wyoming up into Montana.

Eula Wulfjen Kendrick was pretty, spunky, and stylish. At age seventeen, this finishing school–educated young woman "set her cap" for thirty-three-year-old John B. Kendrick, and she married him the following year. Eula Kendrick was the kind of woman who could, with equal grace, brand a calf or preside over an elegant dinner party. This is her recipe for ice cream mousse served in tiny flowerpots and decorated with fresh edible flowers.

Eula Kendrick's Ice Cream Mousse

1 ¼ cups sugar

1 teaspoon cider vinegar

2 large eggs, separated

Juice of 1 lemon (2 to 3 tablespoons)

1 pint heavy cream

1 teaspoon vanilla extract

½ cup crushed strawberries, peaches, or other fruit (optional)

Cocoa powder

Sprigs of sweet pea or roses, for garnish

In a large, heavy saucepan, combine the sugar, vinegar, and ¹/₂ cup of water. Bring to a boil and cook over medium-high heat for 8 to 10 minutes, until the mixture becomes a thick syrup.

Meanwhile, beat the egg yolks until pale yellow in a mixing bowl. Remove the syrup from the heat, stir in the lemon juice, and gradually whisk the syrup into the yolks, taking care not to scramble the eggs. Place the yolk mixture in the top of a double boiler and set it over a pan of simmering water. Cook 2 to 3 minutes, stirring constantly, until thickened. Place the top of the double boiler in a pan of cold water and allow the custard to cool.

In a large, clean metal mixing bowl, beat the egg whites until stiff but not dry. In a separate bowl, whip the cream until it forms soft peaks, then add the vanilla. Gently fold the lemon juice and fruit (if desired) into the custard, then fold the custard mixture and whipped cream into the beaten whites. Freeze in an ice-cream machine as the manufacturer directs or place in the freezer for several hours, stirring 3 or more times, until the mixture is solid.

Spoon the frozen mousse into 6 to 8 clean miniature glazed or plastic flowerpots and return to the freezer until ready to serve. Just before serving, dust the tops with cocoa powder and insert a sprig of sweet pea or a single rose in each pot.

Serves 6 to 8

THE HOMESTEADING
ERA

4

*F*OLLOWING THE COWBOYS and cattlemen into the American West were the homesteaders, who wanted to build houses and till the land. Cattlemen called the homesteaders "nesters" and resented them claiming public land or open cattle range for their farms. But under the Homestead Act of 1862, any American citizen who was twenty-one years old or the head of a family, or had served fourteen days in the U.S. Army or Navy, could file for one hundred sixty acres of federal land. In 1866, Confederate veterans also became eligible. Each homesteader who resided on or farmed the claim for five years received title to the land. A homesteader could buy his claim for $1.25 per acre after living on it for six months, but few could afford to do so.

Many people in Kansas and Nebraska filed homestead claims soon after the act became law, but the real surge of homesteaders did not occur until after the Civil War, when many people came west to forget the battles and to search for better lives. By the late 1860s, however, much of the government land in the moist sections of the Middle West had already been sold or granted to railroads. Thus homesteaders were forced to push farther west, into the more arid and more isolated sections of the generally treeless Great Plains.

The men, women, and children who homesteaded lived simply. They built their houses of sod and fueled their fires with buffalo chips, cow chips, or corn cobs. With experience, they could gauge the heat from these fuels so exactly that they could turn out as fine an angel food cake as can be made in the most elaborate modern oven.

Many homesteaders considered themselves lucky if they had an iron kettle, two or three pans, a wood stove, and a water bucket—few of them had wells and most had to carry water from the nearest spring or creek.

The barrenness and the isolation of the Great Plains combined to create countless human hardships, and homesteaders quickly learned to make do or do without. After a time a really lucky homesteader might have a milk cow, some chickens, a garden, and perhaps some hogs to sell or butcher during the cooler months. Neighbors often came together to help with the butchering because there was much heavy lifting, and they were usually given portions of the meat in exchange for equal portions when the time came to butcher their livestock.

Nearly every homesteader had to improvise, salvage, and substitute one thing for another. "Apple" pies were sometimes made out of soda crackers, and people learned to stretch their supply of coffee by adding barley or rye that had been parched in the oven and ground in a coffee mill. When cream was added, the coffee had a pleasing taste. When sugar was not available, sorghum molasses was the common sweetener and there are accounts of settlers boiling watermelon juice into syrup to sweeten dishes

The prairie itself provided some wild foods. During the summer, wild greens formed a large part of the diet. Buffalo peas were pickled, and sheep sorrel was sweetened with molasses and made into a tart pie that was keenly relished. Wild game—including rabbits, wild turkeys, prairie chickens, ducks, and geese—occasionally provided meat for the dinner table. But homesteaders grew very tired of their monotonous diet of cornbread, sorghum, and salt pork.

The staple fruits were dried peaches and apples. In fact, everything that could be was dried—including rhubarb, which was cut into one-inch-thick slices, strung on a thread, and hung to dry in the sun. Pumpkin was sliced thin or cut up into small dice and strung for drying. The flesh became dark and leathery, but when soaked in water at Thanksgiving or Christmas, it made a fair pumpkin pie.

Corn was another staple in the diet of most homesteaders. During the 1860s they looked for as many different ways to prepare corn as possible. Countless corn recipes include mush or hasty pudding, samp (yellow corn, crushed but not ground and boiled), corn on the cob, dried corn, hominy, corn cakes, apple corn bread (cornmeal and other ingredients mixed with raw apples and baked), corn dodgers, pumpkin Indian loaf (a kind of corn cake made of cornmeal, pumpkin, and molasses), corn bread, corn muffins, and griddle cakes. When neighbors came calling, there was popped corn and sorghum taffy. Mothers often sent their children off to school with corn bread and molasses sandwiches.

During the early years, canning was uncommon. The usual method of preserving food was by means of a salt brine. Some homesteaders kept tomatoes submerged in barrels of strong brine. When they were needed for a meal, a few tomatoes were taken from the barrel and soaked in cold water, which was changed frequently until the brine was soaked out. The tomatoes were then cooked.

After flour became more readily available, flapjacks or pancakes served with sorghum became a favorite dish, as was a gravy made by browning lard and flour together in a cast-iron frying pan, adding water, and bringing the mixture to a boil. White flour biscuits were rare treats and were often eaten like cake.

The homesteaders who proved up on their claims were a hardy lot. Many of their descendants still reside on family homesteads, but their lives are not as hard and their food is not as bland as the fare of their ancestors. Good nutrition prevails today, but the simple food of the early homesteaders is an enduring part of the heritage of the American West and is now enjoyed by countless Americans.

—David Dary

Potato Doughnuts

In doing research on old Wyoming recipes, I was fortunate to speak with Martha Fehlman, author of *Martha's Pioneer Cookbook* (see Mail-Order Sources). Doughnut-making has a long history in Martha Fehlman's family. In 1890, when the family wintered in Green River, Wyoming, Martha's grandmother Martha Whitman made homemade doughnuts and coffee to sell to railroad passengers. Martha Fehlman became famous for her potato doughnuts when she and her late husband, Byron Fehlman, owned and operated the Covered Wagon Motel and Snack Shop in Cody, Wyoming. This is her recipe.

DOUGHNUTS

2 (¼-ounce) packages active dry yeast

2 cups milk

1 cup sugar

½ cup vegetable shortening

1 cup mashed potatoes

3 large eggs, beaten

½ teaspoon vanilla extract

½ teaspoon ground cinnamon

8 cups unbleached all-purpose flour
  (approximately)

Vegetable shortening, for frying

GLAZE

1 ½ cups confectioners' sugar

1 teaspoon vanilla extract

To make the doughnuts, stir the yeast into ¹/₄ cup of warm water. Let stand 5 minutes.

In a saucepan, scald the milk and add the sugar, shortening, and mashed potatoes. Place the mixture in a mixing bowl and stir in the beaten eggs. Add the vanilla, cinnamon, and yeast mixture. Add the flour one-fourth at a time and, working with a strong wooden spoon, beat to make a smooth dough. Cover and let rise until the dough holds an impression when touched, 1 to 1 ¹/₄ hours.

Lightly roll out a portion of dough until it is ¹/₄-inch thick. Cut out doughnuts with a doughnut cutter. Repeat with the remaining dough. Cover and let rise until each doughnut doubles in size, about 45 minutes.

Fry in fat or vegetable shortening heated to 375° F and at least 1-inch deep. Lower the doughnuts into the hot oil one at a time and cook about 3 minutes, turning the doughnuts when brown on one side.

Drain on paper towels (see Note) and then dip in glaze. Reheat the oil to 375° F between batches so the doughnuts won't absorb too much fat.

Makes approximately 4 dozen

To make the glaze, mix ¹/₄ cup of water, the confectioners' sugar, and the vanilla. If the glaze becomes thick enough to crack, thin it with a little water.

Unglazed doughnuts may be frozen. Glaze them when ready to eat.

NOTE: Here is a doughnut making tip from Martha: Remove the fried doughnuts from the hot fat with a fork, dunk them into boiling water, and then place them on waxed paper. Be sure to wipe the fork with a folded paper towel before removing each doughnut from the hot fat. When you're finished, you will be amazed at the amount of fat in the water. The doughnuts will taste better and keep fresh much longer and the calories won't add up so fast.

Butterscotch Rolls

In 1874 William Mathew Ferguson, his wife, Martha, and their three daughters arrived in Cheyenne, Wyoming Territory. The family's original destination was Colorado, but by the time they reached Cheyenne they had run out of money. To finance the remainder of the journey, Martha Ferguson began to bake and sell bread. There was such demand for her bread and rolls that the family decided to stay in Cheyenne, where they established the first bakery. To gather fuel for the bakery ovens, William Ferguson drove each week to a picturesque wooded area west of Cheyenne. He was enchanted by the beauty of this unsettled land and impressed with its wonderful grass and water. In 1876 he bought a few Longhorn cattle and moved his family out of Cheyenne to a homestead. Today, the fifth generation of Fergusons is living on the ranch, continuing the family ranching tradition.

It has been said that eating one of Dorothy Ferguson's butterscotch rolls is like dying and going to heaven. We agree and thank Mrs. Ferguson for giving us her recipe.

DOUGH

¾ cup milk

½ cup butter or margarine, softened

½ cup sugar

2 teaspoons salt

2 (¼-ounce) packages active dry yeast

1 large egg

4 cups unbleached all-purpose flour

TOPPING

¼ cup corn syrup

2 tablespoons butter or margarine

1 cup butterscotch bits

½ cup pecans

⅔ cup melted margarine or butter

⅔ cup firmly packed brown sugar

½ cup raisins

To make the dough, bring the milk just to a simmer in a large saucepan. Stir in the butter, sugar, and salt. Remove from the heat and cool until lukewarm.

In a warmed large bowl, dissolve the yeast in ½ cup of warm water. Stir in the lukewarm milk mixture, the egg, and half of the flour. Beat until smooth. Stir in the remaining flour to make a stiff dough. Cover tightly with foil and refrigerate up to 24 hours.

When ready to form the rolls, make the filling. In a small saucepan, combine the corn syrup, 1 tablespoon of water, and the butter. Bring to a boil, stirring constantly. Remove from the heat and stir in the butterscotch bits until they melt. Spread the mixture in a greased 9-by-13-inch baking pan and sprinkle with the pecans.

Divide the chilled dough in half. Roll each half into a 9-by-12-inch rectangle. Brush each rectangle with the melted margarine and sprinkle each half with brown sugar and raisins. Roll up tightly, starting from one of the 9-inch sides. Cut each roll into nine 1-inch slices. Place the slices in the pan on top of the butterscotch mixture. Cover and allow to rise in a warm area until doubled in size, about 1 hour.

Preheat the oven to 350° F. Bake the rolls on the middle rack of the oven for about 30 minutes, until golden brown. Serve warm.

Makes 15 to 18 rolls

Quick Baking Powder Biscuits

My grandmother May Ketcham Cox was always on the go. As a young woman she taught country school and thought nothing of making a fifty-mile trip on horseback to return home for long weekends. She was a fine horsewoman, equally at ease riding sidesaddle or astride, and a crack shot who often returned home with a couple of rabbits slung across her saddle.

These Baking Powder Biscuits were one of her favorite recipes. A woman ahead of her time, she was not one to linger in the kitchen if there was a party to attend or a horse to ride.

1 ¾ cups unbleached all-purpose flour

2 ½ teaspoons double-acting baking powder (2 teaspoons at high altitudes)

1 teaspoon salt

3 tablespoons chilled butter

3 tablespoons chilled vegetable shortening

1 cup milk

Preheat the oven to 450° F.

Sift the flour, baking powder, and salt into a mixing bowl. With a pastry blender or 2 knives, cut in the butter and shortening until the mixture resembles coarse cornmeal. Add the milk all at once and stir the dough for barely 1 minute. Drop the dough by tablepoonfuls onto an ungreased baking sheet. Bake for 12 to 15 minutes, until lightly browned.

Makes 1 dozen

Cream Biscuits

In the late 1860s my great-grandfather Benjamin Franklin Ketcham started the first dairy in the young town of Cheyenne. He delivered milk and cream daily to housewives who would bring their fruit jars or pots out to the milk wagon to be filled.

When there was extra cream, my great-grandmother Zelda Alversta Ketcham would sometimes make these Cream Biscuits as a special treat for her family. When making biscuits, she often patted the dough into a rectangle and cut it into squares to save time.

2 cups unbleached all-purpose flour

3 teaspoons baking powder (2 teaspoons at high altitudes)

2 teaspoons sugar

½ teaspoon salt

⅓ cup butter

1 cup heavy whipping cream or ⅔ cup milk

Preheat the oven 375° F.

Sift the flour, baking powder, sugar, and salt into a mixing bowl. Cut in the butter. Add the cream gradually, until a soft dough is formed.

Place the dough on a lightly floured board and knead for 1 minute. Pat the dough into a rectangle about ³/₄ inch thick and use a sharp knife to cut it into 3- to 4-inch squares. Place the biscuits about 1¹/₂ inches apart on a lightly greased baking sheet. Bake for about 20 minutes, until golden brown.

Makes 12

Sour Milk Pancakes

Martha Fehlman is a remarkable woman with a fascinating family history. At the age of ninety-one, having lost the sight in one eye, this author of two cookbooks still lives alone in her house in Powell, Wyoming, and maintains a magnificent rose garden with more than 100 varieties. To share their beauty with others, Mrs. Fehlman gives the fragrant blooms to the local cafe, where townspeople gather and summer visitors often stop.

She has been kind enough to share with us her recipe for old-fashioned sour milk (she now uses buttermilk) pancakes.

2 cups unbleached all-purpose flour

2 tablespoons sugar

1 ½ teaspoons baking soda (1 teaspoon in high altitudes)

1 teaspoon salt

2 cups sour milk (see Appendix) or buttermilk

2 tablespoons butter, melted

2 large eggs, well beaten

Butter and maple syrup

Sift the flour, sugar, baking soda, and salt together into a mixing bowl. Add the milk and stir lightly. Add the butter and fold in the eggs.

Drop the batter by large spoonfuls onto a hot, ungreased griddle. When bubbles form all over the top, turn the pancakes and cook until golden brown on the other side. Serve with butter and maple syrup.

Makes 12 to 15 (5- to 6-inch) pancakes

Tuda Crews' Pecan Bread

Tuda Libby Crews grew up on a ranch in northeastern New Mexico. As a girl, Tuda found cleaning barns and raising 4-H steers preferable to boring kitchen work. Consequently, she had never cooked a meal when she married Jack Crews and moved to Wyoming. Common sense told her that if she could read, she could cook—and cook she does. She and Jack have built their own chuck wagon and now compete in chuck-wagon cook-offs throughout the West. Like many cooks living in the country, Tuda has learned to improvise. This delicious bread recipe was invented when she ran out of raisins and threw some pecans into her bread dough.

2 (¼-ounce) packages active dry yeast

¾ cup honey

¼ cup butter, melted

4 cups stone-ground whole wheat flour

5 to 6 cups unbleached all-purpose flour

2 teaspoons salt

2 cups pecan halves

Measure 3 cups of warm water into the large mixing bowl of a heavy-duty electric mixer and stir in the dry yeast. Let stand 5 minutes, until the yeast dissolves. When tiny bubbles appear, add the honey and melted butter. Add the whole wheat flour and 1 cup of the all-purpose flour, beating well after each addition with the paddle attachment. Stir in the salt and pecan halves. Change to the dough hook attachment and continue mixing and adding the remaining all-purpose flour until a stiff dough forms that cleans the flour from the side of the bowl.

Turn out the dough onto a floured surface and knead until smooth. Rub the dough lightly with butter and put it back in the mixing bowl. Cover with a clean kitchen towel and let rise about 1 hour, until doubled in bulk.

Turn the dough out onto a lightly floured surface and cut in half. Gently knead each ball of dough into a smooth rectangle. Using a serrated knife, cut 2 slits about 1 inch deep lengthwise across the top of each loaf. Place each loaf in a greased large loaf pan.

Allow the loaves to rise for about 45 minutes, or until almost doubled in bulk. While the loaves are rising, preheat the oven to 350° F.

Place the risen loaves on the middle rack of the oven and bake for about 50 minutes, or until crusty and golden brown. Remove from the oven and cool on a rack. Brush the top of the hot loaves with a little butter.

To bake the bread over a campfire, after the first rising, put the dough into 2 well-greased 10-inch Dutch ovens. Remember to grease the insides of the lids. Cover and let rise to the top of the lid. Place the Dutch ovens over a bed of hot coals and arrange hot coals evenly over the lid. Cook for 45 minutes, turning the Dutch oven a quarter turn every 10 minutes to prevent hot spots, until the crust has turned a golden brown and a thump on the top of the loaf produces a hollow sound. Remove the loaves from the Dutch ovens and serve.

Yields 2 large loaves

Montana Beef Pasties

In the early 1900s Butte, Montana, was an international town with English, Irish, Welsh, Italian, Finnish, and Chinese neighborhoods. Miners, employed by the powerful Anaconda Copper Mining Company, worked together in the mines but maintained their ethnic identities. Among the English and Welsh miners, meat pasties were a popular lunch dish, one that could be carried down into the mines.

Mining and ranching are the two main industries in Montana. Shelly Van Haur, of the Van Haur Polled Hereford Ranch near Hilger, Montana, grew up outside of Butte. Her father, Peter Jackson, is a long-time cattle rancher, and Shelly married a rancher, but like many Montanans, her family also has ties to mining. Shelly's maternal grandmother, Cora Pierce, raised chickens and sold and delivered eggs to the residents of Butte. Among her customers was the Welsh cook at Garner's Cafe, who was famous for her beef pasties. The cook gave this recipe to Shelly's grandmother and Shelly has shared it with us. We recommend serving the pasties with gravy or ketchup.

2–3 cups diced cooked roast beef

1 cup diced cooked (boiled or baked) potatoes

1 large onion, peeled and diced

3 carrots, diced

1 to 1½ cups leftover beef gravy

2 tablespoons chopped fresh parsley

1 garlic clove, peeled and minced

1 teaspoon salt

¼ teaspoon ground black pepper

1 double recipe of pie dough (see page 174)

1 egg beaten with 1 tablespoon water

Preheat the oven to 400° F.

In a large bowl, combine the beef, potatoes, onion, carrots, gravy, parsley, garlic, salt, and pepper.

On a lightly floured surface, roll the pie dough into 6 to 8 eight-inch rounds about ¼ inch thick. Place about 1 cup of the meat mixture on half of each circle and fold the other half over to enclose the filling. Place on a baking sheet. Brush the edges with the beaten egg and seal, pressing with the tines of a fork. With a small sharp knife, cut a small slit in the top of each pasty. Brush the tops with the beaten egg. Bake for about 1 hour, until golden brown.

Makes 6 to 8 pasties

Oxtail Soup

Oxtail soup and stew—thrifty, old-fashioned recipes—are being rediscovered by modern cooks in search of deep, satisfying flavors. The bones produce a broth with a rich flavor and the meat is succulent. This simple recipe was given to us by Gertrude DeMartine of Pueblo, Colorado, who learned to make oxtail soup as a young bride in the 1930s. At that time, the DeMartine family was living on a small ranch near Walsenburg, Colorado. They cultivated a large garden and raised cattle and other animals for food. When an animal was slaughtered, no part was wasted. Oxtails and other bones were boiled to make a broth to which vegetables from the garden were added. This inexpensive but nourishing soup provided a hearty meal for the growing family.

3 pounds oxtails

2 garlic cloves, peeled

2 teaspoons salt

½ teaspoon ground black pepper

3 red potatoes, peeled and cubed

3 carrots, peeled and cut into 1-inch pieces

2 celery stalks, strings removed and cut into 1-inch pieces

12 boiling onions, about 1-inch in diameter, or 3 small onions, peeled and quartered

Trim the excess fat from the oxtails. Place them in a heavy 5-quart pot with water to cover. Crush the garlic and add to the pot. Cover and bring to a boil over high heat. Reduce the heat to medium and continue to boil for about 5 hours, until the meat is tender. Remove any foam as it forms on the surface and add boiling water as needed to keep the oxtails covered.

When the meat is tender, add the potatoes, carrots, celery, and onions and cook 20 to 30 minutes, until the vegetables are tender and the meat is falling off the bones.

Serves 6

Pitchfork Fondue for a Crowd

There are few more dramatic and tasty ways to serve up steaks for a party than a Montana steak-fry. The basic idea is similar to a traditional beef fondue. The difference is one of scale—the Montana version involves a large cauldron of bubbling hot beef fat, T-bone steaks, and a pitchfork!

Obviously, safety precautions must be taken if you want to try this. The hardwood or charcoal fire should be built in a pit about 1½ feet deep in an area cleared of grass and brush. The pit should be wide enough to allow space for the cook to regulate the fire after the pot is placed on top. A stable metal grate to set over the fire pit is essential, as is a cast-iron cauldron with a flat bottom (see Mail-Order Sources). When deep-frying, the pot should never be more than half full of fat. Whether you are rendering suet or heating vegetable oil, it should be done slowly while the fire is carefully monitored. A fire extinguisher is always a good idea when cooking and a lid or sheet of metal large enough to cover the pot and smother the flames is important in case the fat catches fire. You can throw salt on an oil fire to smother the flames, but never try to douse it with water, because that will only spread the fire. Serve the steaks with your favorite steak sauce, beans, green salad, and hot biscuits.

5 gallons rendered beef suet or cooking oil

6 to 8 slices bread, for testing

24 T-bone steaks (1 to 1½ inches thick)

Salt or seasoned salt

Ground black pepper

ACCOMPANIMENTS

Ketchup and assorted steak sauces

Ranch Frijoles (see page 32), King Ranch Beans (see page 89), or Chuck-Wagon Beans (see page 82)

Green salad

Hot biscuits

Place the fat in a 10- to 12-gallon cast-iron cauldron with a flat bottom set on a grate over a fire pit filled with hot coals. Heat the fat slowly and carefully. When a slice of bread lowered into the pot browns in 60 seconds, the temperature should have reached about 375° F, the proper temperature for frying the steaks.

While the fat is heating, season the steaks with salt and pepper. Dip the tines of three or four clean pitchforks into the oil so that the meat won't stick and then thread two to three steaks securely onto each fork.

When the frying temperature is reached, lower one fork at a time into the hot fat to cook the steaks. The steaks should be cooked rare in 1½ to 2 minutes, medium-rare in 2 to 2½ minutes, and medium in 3 minutes. Carefully lift the steaks out of the cauldron and use tongs to remove them to serving pans lined with crumpled paper towels. Thread the remaining steaks on the pitchforks and be sure to allow the fat to come to the proper frying temperature between batches.

Serves 24 to 48

Edna Jones' Pot o' Beans with Pink Applesauce

Ranch women are usually prepared to feed extra mouths with very little notice. Since the days of the open range, when cowboys "rode the chuck line," and depended on the hospitality of ranchers for food and shelter, it has been customary to feed ranch hands and neighbors who are helping with ranch work and to offer at least a cup of coffee or a glass of lemonade to anyone who stops by.

Mrs. L. L. (Edna) Jones of Garden City, Kansas, maintains that between 1917—when the Jones ranch was established—and 1952—when they dispersed their award-winning registered Hereford herd—she "packed more box lunches for men moving cattle than any ranch wife in Kansas." When the cowboys were working closer to home and could come in for a proper dinner, she often served her famous short ribs and beans with cool pink applesauce, hot cornbread slathered with butter and honey, and tall glasses of iced tea. It is no wonder that the Jones ranch was a favorite destination for friends and neighbors.

Pot o' Beans

2 to 3 pounds beef short ribs

1 pound dried pinto beans, picked and rinsed

2 teaspoons salt

Preheat oven to 350° F.

To cook the ribs, place the short ribs in a shallow baking pan and bake, uncovered, $1^1/_2$ to 2 hours, until browned and tender. Pour off the juices and reserve. Place the ribs on paper towels to absorb the excess fat.

Skim off the fat from the top of the reserved juices. Add water to the juices to make 12 cups of liquid for cooking the beans. In a heavy 10-quart kettle, combine the beans, the 12 cups of liquid, and salt. Bring to a boil and simmer 2 to 3 minutes. Cover and remove from the heat. Allow to stand for 1 hour.

Add the ribs to the kettle and bring to a boil. Reduce the heat and simmer for about $1^1/_2$ hours, until the beans are tender. (At higher altitudes, allow 1 to 2 hours longer to cook the beans.) The broth should be cooked down enough to make a sauce.

Serves 6 to 8

Pink Applesauce

8 Jonathan or other tart apples (about 2 pounds), cored, peeled (reserve peels), and thinly sliced

$^1/_2$ cup sugar, or to taste

In a medium saucepan, place the apples, $^1/_2$ cup of water, and the reserved peels. Bring to a boil and simmer 15 to 20 minutes, until fork tender, stirring occasionally. Remove the peels and add the sugar to the hot applesauce, stirring until dissolved. Serve warm. The applesauce should be chunky.

Makes 3 to 4 cups

Rich Riced Potatoes

Some cooks make a virtue out of lumpy mashed potatoes, saying that lumps prove they are homemade, but my grandmother May Cox knew better. When asked how she produced such fluffy potatoes, Grandma just smiled and said she made them like everyone else did. Although an old-fashioned wooden potato masher hung in her kitchen, a ricer was her secret weapon. When riced—or pressed through a food mill or coarse strainer—mashed potatoes are lump-free and lighter in texture. For richness and flavor, whisk in a little heated cream or milk and a chunk of butter as my grandmother did. The only seasonings needed are salt, pepper, and a sprinkling of paprika for color.

4 medium baking potatoes

Salt

⅓ to ½ cup light cream, milk, or low-fat milk, warmed

1 to 3 tablespoons butter

Ground black pepper

Paprika (optional)

Scrub the potatoes and cut out any eyes and blemishes. Peel and cut them into halves or quarters. If preparing in advance, place potatoes in a bowl with cold water to cover.

In a large saucepan, bring 4 cups of lightly salted water to a boil. Add the potatoes and boil for about 20 minutes, or until they are tender when pierced with a knife. Drain the potatoes thoroughly. Put them through a ricer into a saucepan placed over low heat. Gradually whisk in the hot cream and butter and season to taste with salt and pepper. Sprinkle lightly with paprika and serve immediately.

If you must prepare them ahead, spoon the potatoes into a buttered baking dish, cover with a thin film of cream, dot with butter, and place in a preheated 300° F oven for up to 1 hour before serving. Mix well just before you serve.

Serves 4 to 6

Plains and Prairie Fried Chicken

When frying chicken, it is important to watch it carefully and turn the pieces often so they don't burn. Adjust the heat so the fat remains hot, but does not smoke or begin to darken. When turning the pieces, use tongs, not a fork that will pierce the chicken and release juices. The two recipes that follow are quite different, but both are good. Serve either version with a gravy such as Trail Drive and Bunk House Cream Gravy (see page 75).

Montana Fried Chicken

In the early 1880s, the well-funded but shorthanded cattle ranches on the northern Plains lured Texas cowboys to Wyoming, Montana, and the Dakotas with higher wages and better grub than they could expect in most southern outfits. This old Montana ranch recipe for extra-crispy fried chicken could turn most cowboy's heads!

1 young frying chicken (2½ to 3 pounds)
2 large eggs, beaten with 2 tablespoons water
1 cup unbleached all-purpose flour
½ teaspoon salt

¼ to ½ teaspoon ground black pepper
¼ teaspoon paprika or cayenne pepper (optional)
½ to ¾ cup butter
½ to ¾ cup lard or vegetable shortening

To cut the chicken into serving pieces, remove the wings and legs with a sharp knife. Divide each leg into a thigh and a drumstick. Split the breast horizontally at the base of the wishbone and, if it is large, split the larger lower portion again vertically. Split the back in half and, if desired, add the neck. You should end up with 11 to 13 serving pieces, plus the giblets.

Wash the chicken pieces under cold running water and pat dry. Place the egg mixture in a shallow bowl and place the flour, salt, pepper, and paprika in a clean brown paper bag. Coat 1 to 2 pieces of the chicken at a time with the egg mixture, then drop them into the bag and shake to coat with the flour mixture. If the chicken is not completely coated, repeat the process. Arrange the coated chicken pieces with their sides not touching on a baking sheet lined with paper towels and allow the coating to set while you heat the butter and lard.

Place the butter and lard in a deep 12- to 14-inch cast-iron skillet. Heat the fat over medium-high heat. When melted it should be about 1 inch deep. Add more butter and lard if necessary. The temperature for frying is right when a small cube of bread dropped in the hot fat turns golden brown in 60 seconds, or when a deep-frying thermometer immersed in the fat registers 375° F.

Carefully place the chicken, skin side down, in the hot fat. Do not crowd the pan or allow the pieces to touch or they won't fry properly. Do not cover the skillet. Fry the chicken, turning the pieces often, until golden-brown on both sides, 20 to 30 minutes, depending on the size of the pieces. Cook the dark meat slightly longer than the breast pieces. Remove the chicken as it is done and place it in a pan lined with crumpled paper towels to drain.

Serves 4

Grandma Hubbard's Batter-Fried Chicken

The Hubbard family of Nunn, Colorado, has a wonderful old-fashioned fried-chicken recipe that has been handed down for at least four generations.

Kate Walker, Jim Hubbard's grandmother, came to Sharon Springs, Kansas, from Missouri as a mail-order bride in the late 1800s. In those days everything a homesteader might need, from a house to a wife, could be found in the Sears Roebuck catalog. After "proving up" on his claim, Grandpa Hubbard sold his homestead at Sharon Springs and started working for the Southern Pacific Railroad. The rails took the Hubbard family west to Colorado.

Jim remembers his grandmother as a small, spirited woman who could often be found in her garden, wearing a long dress, apron, and sunbonnet. She was a great cook, but strict. Meals in the Hubbard household were served promptly at 6:00 A.M., 12:00 P.M., and 6:00 P.M., and woe to any latecomers!

1 young frying chicken (2½ to 3 pounds), cut into serving pieces

6 large eggs, beaten

½ cup unbleached all-purpose flour

¼ to ½ teaspoon salt

½ to ¾ teaspoon black pepper

3 cups bread crumbs

Vegetable shortening, for frying

Soak the chicken pieces for at least 1 hour—preferably overnight—in lightly salted ice water to cover.

Place the beaten eggs in one small bowl, the flour combined with the salt and pepper in another, and the bread crumbs in another dish. Remove the chicken pieces from the water and dip first in the egg, then in the seasoned flour, then again in the egg, and finally in the bread crumbs. Set the coated pieces aside on a baking sheet lined with paper towels; do not allow the sides to touch. Allow the coating to set while you heat the shortening.

Place enough shortening in a 12- to 14-inch cast-iron skillet to be ½ inch deep when melted. Place the skillet over medium-high heat. The temperature for frying is right when a small cube of bread dropped in the hot fat turns golden brown in 60 seconds, or when a deep-frying thermometer immersed in the fat registers 375° F.

When the fat is hot, carefully place the chicken in the pan, skin-side-down. Fry uncovered for 10 to 15 minutes, or until the chicken is golden brown on one side. Turn the pieces with tongs and cook partially covered, with the lid askew, for 15 to 20 minutes, or until the chicken is golden brown and cooked through.

Carefully pour ¼ cup of water into the pan and remove from the heat. Steam should rise from the pan. Quickly cover the skillet and place over low heat for 5 to 10 minutes to steam; the shorter time will produce crisper chicken.

Serves 4

Sam Arnold's Buffalo Drive Feed

When Sam Arnold described the "feed" he put on when he was "Cookie" on a buffalo drive in Colorado's San Louis Valley (see page 9), it made our mouths water! We had to have those recipes, and Sam was kind enough to oblige.

Sam's Buffalo Burgers

Buffalo meat has less than 2 percent fat and a good burger needs at least 12 percent. So, have your butcher add buffalo, beef, or pork fat when he grinds the buffalo meat. Do not, I repeat, do not pat or squash the burgers while they're cooking. If you do, you will squeeze important juices from them, making them dry and mean!

9 pounds coarsely ground buffalo meat

Salt and black pepper, to taste

20 large hamburger buns, preferably sourdough

1 quart mayonnaise

2 8-ounce bottles Chili Sauce

20 roasted, peeled, and seeded green chiles, chopped

20 very thin slices sweet onion, such as Vidalia or Texas

Form the ground buffalo into six ounce patties. (A tuna can with top and bottom cut out makes a good form.) Grill the patties to medium-rare or medium, about 10 minutes. While cooking, season to taste with salt and pepper.

Open the hamburger buns and place face down on the grill to toast lightly.

Mix the mayonnaise with the chili sauce and dress buns with the sauce mixture. Place a burger in each bun and garnish with some green chile and a slice of onion.

Makes 20 burgers

Sam's Buffalo-Drive Taters

The huge pans used on trail drives can hold enough to serve twenty cowboys (see Mail-Order Sources), but the amounts called for in this dish can be adjusted to fit the size of your frying pans. If you want to be fancy, garnish each plate with parsley.

12 pounds white potatoes

8 large yellow onions

8 pounds medium- to thick-cut bacon

2 quarts chopped roasted green chiles

2 quarts white shoepeg corn kernels

2 tablespoons seasoning salt

3 tablespoons coarsely ground black pepper

Boil the potatoes until cooked, let cool, and then peel and slice them. Cut the onions into thick slices, chop them coarsely, and set aside.

Cover the bottom of a large frying pan with strips of bacon. Continue making layers in a cross-hatch pattern until all the bacon has been used. Place the pan over a hot fire. When the bottom layer is cooked, turn the bacon over.

Add all the onions and let them cook in the bacon drippings for a few minutes. Add the potatoes and cover the pan. Let cook for about 4 minutes, then begin to turn the mixture over with a spatula. When about halfway browned, add the chiles and corn. Season to taste with the seasoning salt and pepper. Continue to turn the mixture in the pan until nicely browned, then serve.

Serves 20

Betty Cox's Rib Roast of Beef with Yorkshire Pudding and Horseradish Sauce

At the Wyoming Angus Ranch near Cheyenne, rib roast served with Yorkshire pudding and horseradish sauce is a favorite menu for special occasions. There are few women who cook a rib roast as well as Betty Cox, and few men who carve it as well as Mark Cox, and I'm not just saying that because they're my parents!

Like many ranchers, my parents have always raised their own beef and pride themselves on producing prime quality, the highest rating of the USDA. Their steers are raised on grass and "finished" for one to two months on a diet of corn. At the stockyard the carcass is hung in a special refrigerated room at a temperature of between 34° F and 39° F for five to six weeks to age before being cut up. My father is a good meat cutter and he works closely with the butcher to make sure that steaks and roasts are cut to his taste.

Since they receive a whole beef at a time, my parents have their beef quick-frozen at the packing plant. My mother has learned through experience that if a roast is frozen it should be rubbed with seasonings and cooked when it is still frozen. If you thaw it, you lose the juices. When cooking a frozen roast, simply add ten minutes more per pound to the time suggested in the recipe.

When cooking any roast, it is a good idea to use a meat thermometer for accuracy. Remember that after you remove the roast from the oven it continues to cook. When purchasing a standing rib roast, ask the butcher to saw through the backbone at the base of each rib and to cut the rib bones to an even length to make carving easier.

Many people are intimidated by the thought of carving a roast, and they find the idea of doing it at the head of the table particularly terrifying. My father admits that it takes a little practice, but notes that most people he has seen struggling with a roast or turkey were trying to carve it using a dull knife on a platter that was too small. He advises investing in a carving board large enough to hold the roast comfortably. Side platters on which to place bones or sliced meat are also handy. Most important of all, buy a good carving knife and keep it sharp!

4 to 6 pound standing rib roast (at least 3 ribs)

Seasoning salt

Freshly ground black pepper

¼ cup beef broth, good quality red wine, or water

Yorkshire Pudding (recipe follows)

Quick and Easy Horseradish Sauce (recipe follows)

Preheat the oven to 350° F.

Rub the roast all over with seasoning salt and pepper and stand it on its rib ends (fat side up) in a shallow roasting pan. Insert a meat thermometer so that the point is centered in the fleshiest portion without touching any bone.

Place the roast on the middle or lower middle rack of the oven and roast, uncovered, allowing about 18 minutes per pound for rare. Keep an eye on the meat thermometer and remove the roast when it reaches 125° F for very rare, 135° F for medium-rare, 145° F for medium, and 160° F for well done.

Place the roast on a warm serving platter or carving board and let it rest for about 20 minutes before carving.

Skim off the excess fat from the top of the pan juices and reserve for the Yorkshire pudding. Add the beef broth to the degreased juices and set the roasting pan over medium-high heat, using two burners if necessary. Bring the juices to a boil, stirring and scraping the bottom of the pan to dissolve the brown meat glaze on the bottom of the pan.

Carve the roast—in thin English-style slices or in ³/₄- to 1-inch thick cattle baron's slices—and serve with the pan juices, Yorkshire Pudding, and Horseradish Sauce.

Serves 4 to 12 (allow ½ to 1 pound per serving)

Yorkshire Pudding

Prepare the Yorkshire pudding while the roast is resting. Cut into squares and serve piping hot from the baking pan. This recipe can be doubled.

4 tablespoons roast beef pan drippings or vegetable oil

3 large eggs

1 cup unbleached all-purpose flour

¾ teaspoon salt

1 cup milk

Place the drippings in a 13-by-9-inch baking pan. Place the pan in the oven and preheat to 450° F.

In a mixing bowl, beat the eggs well. Sift together the flour and salt and stir into the eggs. Gradually add the milk and beat for 2 minutes with a rotary eggbeater. Pour the batter into the preheated pan and bake 25 to 30 minutes, until puffed and golden brown.

Serves 6 to 8

Quick and Easy Horseradish Sauce

¾ cup mayonnaise

¼ cup prepared horseradish

Fresh parsley sprig, for garnish

In a small sauceboat, combine the mayonnaise and horseradish. Top with a small sprig of parsley.

Makes 1 cup

Dakota Golden Pheasant Fricassee

Pheasants were brought to the United States from their native China in the early 1900s and have thrived on the western prairies. South Dakota, "Pheasant Capital of the World," is known for pheasant hunting and preparation.

Mark and Vicky Huls of Salem, South Dakota, are the picture of a busy, active ranching family. They raise cattle and also grow wheat, corn, and hay. Like many modern ranchers, they both also have other full-time jobs. If work and ranching weren't enough, they have seven children as well. With this big family, Vicky always keeps an eye open for easy dishes that appeal to everyone while filling up their teenaged children.

The Huls ranch is a popular place during hunting season, when friends from across the country come to shoot the abundant ringneck pheasants in the pastures and corn stubble. This recipe is an old-fashioned pheasant fricassee as Vicky's grandma might have cooked it. With her busy schedule, Vicky often simplifies the traditional recipe by using canned mushroom soup instead of making a cream sauce. Either version is great when served with wild or white rice, or a mixture of the two.

3 to 4 slices thick-sliced bacon, diced

2 pheasants (3–3¼ pounds each), disjointed for frying

Salt and freshly ground black pepper

2 cups unbleached all-purpose flour

6 tablespoons butter or vegetable oil

½ cup chopped onion

½ pound fresh mushrooms, wiped clean and sliced thin

4 cups chicken broth

1½ cups light cream

2 fresh tomatoes, peeled, seeded, and diced, or 1 (14½-ounce) can diced tomatoes, with juices

2 tablespoons minced fresh parsley (optional)

Preheat the oven to 350° F.

In a large Dutch oven, cook the bacon over medium-low heat until crisp. Remove with a slotted spoon and drain on paper towels. Pour off and discard all but 2 tablespoons of the bacon drippings from the pan.

Season the pheasants to taste with salt and pepper and roll in the flour, shaking off the excess. Reserve any remaining flour. Add 2 tablespoons of the butter to the drippings in the pan and place over medium-high heat. Add the pheasants and brown on all sides, 12 to 15 minutes. If necessary, brown in batches to avoid crowding the pan.

Add the remaining 4 tablespoons butter, the onion, and the mushrooms to the pan and sauté for 1 minute. Stir in the reserved flour and cook, stirring, for about 1 minute. Gradually whisk in the broth and cream and cook, stirring, until the sauce begins to thicken. Return the pheasants and any juices to the pan. Gently stir in the tomatoes. Cover and place in the oven. Bake until the pheasants are fork tender, 1 to 1½ hours. Season to taste with salt and pepper and sprinkle with parsley before serving.

Serves 8 to 10

See photograph, page 134.

Milk-Can Supper

Milk-can suppers are the Western equivalent of clambakes. In the high plains of Wyoming and Colorado they are a popular way of entertaining a crowd during the late summer and early fall when fresh corn is available.

This recipe comes from Leonard Wiggin. The Wiggins, intrepid Bostonians, homesteaded in northeastern Colorado in the 1870s, during the days of the open range and the big roundups. Milk-can suppers at the Wiggin Ranch near Grover, Colorado, are often followed by a fierce but friendly game of "ten-point pitch," the still-popular card game seen in old westerns.

When removing the lid, be careful to avoid the scalding steam. Two strong men wearing heavy oven mitts usually empty the can into the serving containers. We have seen everything from a wooden hog trough to a wheelbarrow to a washtub used as serving vessels. Guests usually serve themselves and move on to a separate table set up with accompaniments.

25 ears sweet corn, shucked (reserve a few husks for lining can)

25 medium red potatoes, scrubbed but unpeeled

3 pounds carrots, peeled and halved

6 medium onions, peeled and quartered (optional)

4 heads green cabbage, cored and quartered (optional)

50 Polish or German sausages, or for a spicier taste include some chorizo sausages

3 to 4 cups beer

A C C O M P A N I M E N T S
Butter or margarine
Sour cream
Tossed green salad
Hot bread or biscuits

To prepare the fire, dig a shallow pit 8 inches deep by 20 inches wide. Place two cement blocks, which will support the milk can, on either side of the pit. Build the fire using about 10 to 15 pieces of hardwood (about $1^{1}/_{2}$ inces in diameter and 15 inches long). When the embers are white hot, the fire is ready. (Continue to add wood little by little to maintain a slow, even temperature while cooking.)

Place a thin layer of corn husks on the bottom of a clean, unrusted 8- or 10-gallon milk can to insulate the food from the fire. Place the potatoes in the can, then add layers of carrots, onions, corn, cabbage, and sausages. If necessary, stuff the sausages into the can. Combine 3 cups of the beer and 3 cups of water and pour into the can. If your can has a lid, place it on

gently to allow some steam to escape. (This is very important as a lid that is jammed on may cause steam to build up and blow both the lid and the contents of the can out the top.) If you do not have a lid, improvise one by placing a doubled sheet of heavy-duty aluminum foil over the top of the can and crimping the edges.

Set the filled milk can on the cement blocks above the fire and cook gently for 1 to $1^{1}/4$ hours. Add more wood to the fire as needed. If the liquid in the can seems to be boiling away, add the remaining 1 cup of beer combined with 1 cup of water. Empty the can into serving containers.

Serves 20 to 25

Federer Spare Ribs and Sauerkraut

My neighbor Joan Anderson remembers that in her family, sauerkraut was always served at big dinners. In the early days it was made in quantity in large crocks and was considered to be a healthy addition to meals.

Joan's grandmother Antonia Brambora was born in 1897 in Bohemia. With her family, she came to America as a child. The Bramboras moved west to Wyoming and, in 1913, Antonia married John Federer, a dashing young man known as a fine hand with horses. The young couple moved to John's homestead north of Cheyenne.

John and Tony, as Antonia was known, had twelve children. When their youngest child was two, John Federer was killed by a runaway team and Tony was left with a large family to raise. With the help of her daughter Frances and her son-in-law Whitey Christenson, Tony raised her young children.

The Christensons ran a dairy and Mrs. Federer raised chickens and sold eggs to customers in Cheyenne. Those were depression years, but the family was always proud that they fed and clothed themselves. Tony Federer overcame hardship and also knew how to laugh. Her children and grandchildren remember her as a wonderful cook who took time to amuse them with stories and to read their fortunes in the cards. This is her recipe for spare ribs and sauerkraut.

4 pounds spare ribs

2 tablespoons butter

½ sliced onion (about ½ cup)

1 tablespoon unbleached all-purpose flour

1 tablespoon sugar

2 (27-ounce) cans sauerkraut

Preheat the oven to 350° F.

Lightly brush a large Dutch oven with oil. Place the pan over medium heat and when hot add the spare ribs. Brown the ribs, turning occasionally, for 10 to 15 minutes. Add ½ cup of water and bring to boil. Cover and place in the oven to bake for 1½ to 2 hours, until the ribs are tender.

In a large skillet over medium heat, melt the butter. Add the onion and sauté for 2 to 3 minutes, until translucent. Stir in the flour and sugar. Cook, stirring, for 2 to 3 minutes, until the mixture is lightly browned. Add the sauerkraut and stir to combine. Remove the ribs from the Dutch oven. Drain off and discard the excess fat. Stir the sauerkraut mixture in the Dutch oven to deglaze. Add the ribs and reheat.

Serves 4 to 6

Oriental Saloon Stew

In the 1870s, as increasing numbers of homesteaders settled in Kansas and Texas, cattlemen in those states saw that the days of the open range were numbered. They began to look north and west to the still open and unsettled land in New Mexico, Arizona, Colorado, Wyoming, and Montana. In Arizona, even the fierce Apaches could not hold back the influx of cattlemen and miners, but up until the 1890s the territory was dangerous.

Even by early Arizona standards, Tombstone was a mining town with a wild reputation. The Oriental Saloon, one of Tombstone's "pleasure palaces," was known as a hangout for cowboys and outlaws. Fights and shootings were common at the Oriental. This recipe for beef stew is adapted from an 1880s recipe given to the uncle of the rodeo champion and cookbook author Wes Medley by a former cook and bartender at the Oriental. The addition of cinnamon, ground chile, cloves, cumin, and crushed red pepper makes this stew a spice- and fire-eater's delight!

2½ to 3 pounds lean beef stew meat, cubed

2 tablespoons unbleached all-purpose flour

1 tablespoon sweet paprika

4 teaspoons ground red chile (preferably New Mexican) or chili powder

2 teaspoons salt

3 tablespoons vegetable oil

2 yellow onions, peeled and sliced (about 3 cups)

1 garlic clove, peeled and minced

1 (28-ounce) can tomatoes, with liquid

1 tablespoon ground cinnamon

½ teaspoon ground cloves

¼ teaspoon ground cumin

¼ to ¾ teaspoon crushed red pepper (optional)

4 potatoes, peeled and cubed

4 carrots, peeled and cut into 1½-inch lengths

Pat the beef cubes dry with paper towels. In a large bowl combine the flour, paprika, 1 teaspoon of the ground chile, and the salt. Add the beef cubes and toss to coat with the seasoned flour.

Heat the oil in a large Dutch oven over medium-high heat. Add the beef cubes in batches and brown on all sides for about 6 to 8 minutes. Add the onions and garlic and cook over medium-low heat for 2 to 3 minutes, until softened. Add the tomatoes, remaining 3 teaspoons ground chile, cinnamon, cloves, cumin, and crushed red pepper, if desired. Reduce the heat to low. Cover and simmer for 2 hours. Add the potatoes and carrots and simmer an additional 30 to 40 minutes, until the beef and vegetables are tender.

Serves 6 to 8

Mother Ward's Famous Gumbo

Mary Evans Ward was fiercely independent, the epitome of a Texas frontier lady. At the Crescent V Ranch in the 1870s she raised eight children, fought off Indians, killed rattlesnakes, kept watch for cattle rustlers, sat out hurricanes, and prepared food for more than thirty plates a day. She was a good shot and a great cook!

The Wards and their friends, the Bennetts from the neighboring Garcitas Ranch, often gathered to feast on Mary Ward's delicious gumbo, made with oysters fresh from Karankaway Bay. If the party was held at Garcitas, family stories describe Mother Ward packing up all eight children and a pot of gumbo in a mule-drawn buggy and crossing the coastal swamps with children bouncing and gumbo sloshing.

Today, Mary Ward's great grandson, John S. Bennett, owns the Crescent V and is a partner in the Garcitas. When the families gather each year for Thanksgiving, the aroma of Mother Ward's famous gumbo wafts through the air and her memory is cherished.

5- to 6-pound stewing hen

1 (44-ounce) can chicken broth

1 teaspoon peppercorns

1 bay leaf

2 large red potatoes, peeled and diced

2 tablespoons uncooked rice

2 tablespoons bread crumbs

1 (15.5-ounce) can chopped tomatoes

1 quart fresh okra, sliced, or 1 (16-ounce) package frozen okra

20 fresh bay oysters, shucked, or 1 (8-ounce) container oysters

¼ cup minced fresh parsley

1 to 2 teaspoons gumbo filé powder

Tabasco sauce

Place the hen in a large kettle. Add broth and enough water to make two quarts. Tie the peppercorns and bay leaf in a small piece of cheesecloth and place in the kettle with the hen. Bring to a boil, reduce the heat to low, and simmer the hen for 1½ to 2½ hours, until almost tender. Skim off and discard any foam that rises to the top. Place the pot in the refrigerator to cool. Skim off and discard the fat that rises to the top.

Remove the chicken meat from the bones, cut in bite-size pieces, and return to the broth. Add the potatoes, rice, bread crumbs, tomatoes, and okra, and stir in up to 1 cup additional boiling water if needed to cover the ingredients. Bring the gumbo to a simmer. Cover and cook until the potatoes and rice are tender. Stir in the oysters and parsley and remove from the heat. Add the filé powder, season to taste with Tabasco, and serve.

Serves 6 to 8

High Plains Barbecue

According to Albert Keester, the only ingredients needed for High Plains Barbecue are great beef, fresh air, salt, and pepper. The Keester family has been preparing barbecue at rodeos and other celebrations for many years and though the basic ingredients are simple, there is a little more to the recipe than that.

In Wyoming and Colorado, barbecue was traditionally cooked in open pits lined with a deep bed of wood embers. The cook used any wood at hand, but often it was old untreated Texas cedar fence posts. When the fire was right, metal grates were placed over the pit. The beef, usually a whole hindquarter with the loin removed, weighing 80 to 100 pounds, was rubbed with salt and pepper and placed fat side down on the grate. It was turned occasionally and cooked slowly for about 10 hours.

The Keesters—and other modern barbecue cooks—have built themselves portable versions of the old pits. Today, metal barrel barbecues on wheels, some large enough to cook a whole hind quarter, can be seen hitched to pickup trucks on their way to celebrations.

Albert Keester uses good-quality hardwood charcoal rather than wood in his barrel cooker. After the initial searing of the beef, he tries to maintain a temperature of between 200° and 300° F. Nowadays, the beef is usually large rib eye or top-round roasts, weighing about 25 pounds each, rather than the more unwieldy hindquarters. Albert offers this recipe so you can duplicate his barbecue at home. Remember that cooking outdoors is not an exact science. Factors such as outdoor air temperature, wind direction, and wind velocity all affect the cooking time.

10 pound rib-eye or top-round roast
Salt and ground black pepper

Rub the roast with salt and pepper to taste. Place the roast on a grill over white-hot coals or a gas grill preheated to hot, and sear on all sides. Cover the grill and partially close the vents to let the fire die down or, if using a gas grill, turn off the central burner and turn down the side burners to medium-low. Cook the beef slowly, allowing 10 to 15 minutes per pound for rare to medium-rare. Turn the roast carefully from time to time, being careful not to pierce the roast and allow juices to escape. Remove the roast from the grill when the temperature registers 10 degrees less than the desired temperature, 140° F for rare and 150° F for medium-rare. Tent the roast loosely with aluminum foil and allow to rest for 10 minutes before carving.

Serves 15 to 20

Grandma Ketcham's Macaroni Casserole

At twenty, Zelda Alvesta traveled from her birthplace in Iowa to the still-wild Wyoming Territory to marry her sweetheart, Benjamin Franklin Ketcham. The young couple set up housekeeping near Cheyenne and started the town's first dairy and meat market. Zelda Ketcham bore 10 children, including my grandmother May Ketcham Cox, and buried the three who died as infants on a hill within view of the house. Years later, when it was discovered that the graveyard was located on land belonging to neighboring Fort Russell, the U.S. Army informed the family that the graves must be moved. Zelda Ketcham moved her rocking chair to the graveyard and sat there day and night with a shotgun in her lap. In the end, the Army reconsidered and the graves were not disturbed.

In addition to being handy with a gun, Zelda Ketcham was a good plain cook. I never got to meet her, but her recipe for macaroni tossed with sour cream and stewed tomatoes and topped with buttered bread crumbs was passed down in the family and remains one of my favorite recipes from childhood.

Salt

8 ounces elbow macaroni

1 pint sour cream

2 (14-ounce) cans tomatoes, with liquid

½ teaspoon ground black pepper

2 tablespoons butter

¾ cup bread crumbs

Preheat the oven to 325° F.

Bring a large pot of lightly salted water to a boil and cook the macaroni until nearly tender. Drain the macaroni well and place it in a 2-quart buttered casserole. Mix in the sour cream, tomatoes, $^1/_2$ teaspoon salt, and the pepper.

In a skillet over medium heat, melt the butter and stir in the bread crumbs, combining well. Sprinkle the buttered crumbs over the macaroni mixture and bake for 20 to 25 minutes, until the sauce is bubbling and the topping is golden brown.

Serves 4 to 6

Marie Ketcham's Molded Lime Salad

There could be an entire book devoted to the role of the molded gelatin salad in ranch cooking. Suffice it to say that I have never been invited to Sunday dinner at a ranch without at least one being served. At church suppers and other "pot luck" events, there is often a whole table covered with a rainbow-colored assortment of gelatin concoctions. In my family, the lime-flavored salad with a hint of horseradish served by Aunt Marie Ketcham was a favorite. Its sweet and savory flavor complements fried chicken and most other meats.

1 (3-ounce) package lemon gelatin

1 (3-ounce) package lime gelatin

1 (20-ounce) can crushed pineapple, with juice

1 (12-ounce) can evaporated milk

1 (8-ounce) container small-curd cottage cheese

1 cup mayonnaise

3 tablespoons prepared horseradish

½ cup chopped walnuts or pecans

Celery and carrot sticks, for garnish

In a mixing bowl, combine the lemon and lime gelatin and 2 cups of hot water and stir until dissolved. Allow the mixture to cool for about 10 minutes, stirring occasionally. Stir in the pineapple and evaporated milk and let stand for 20 minutes.

In a small bowl, combine the cottage cheese, mayonnaise, horseradish, and nuts. Fold into the gelatin mixture. Pour the mixture into a 9-cup mold or two 4½-cup ring molds. Place in the refrigerator to chill until firm, about 1 hour. Gently run a thin-bladed knife around the edge of the mold to loosen. Dip the bottom of the mold briefly into tepid water. Place a serving plate face-down on top of the mold. Carefully invert the mold onto the plate and lift off the mold. If using a ring mold, you may want to fill the center with tender celery branches with leaves attached and carrot sticks.

Serves 10 to 12

Linda Vernon's Pickled Beets

County and state fairs are important annual events for ranch and farm families. Competition in canning, baking, livestock breeding, and showing is taken seriously. Adults and children of all ages spend months in preparation for this opportunity to get together to socialize and show what they have accomplished since the previous year.

When Gordon and I moved back to the ranch, I was asked to act as Culinary Superintendent for the Laramie County Fair, held in Cheyenne in the beginning of August. The recipe below comes from Linda Vernon, Grand Prize Winner in Canning and Preserving for two years in a row. When she is not "putting up" and caring for her husband and young daughter, Linda writes for several local and national publications.

1 gallon medium beets

7 cups sugar

3 cups vinegar

4 tablespoons mustard seed

4 tablespoons mixed pickling spice

Cut the beet tops to within 1 inch of the beets. In a large pot, boil the beets until fork-tender. Slip off the skins and the tops. Slice the beets about 1 inch thick and pack into sterilized hot pint canning jars.

Place the sugar, vinegar, mustard seed, and pickling spice in a large saucepan and bring to a rolling boil. Ladle the boiling liquid into the jars. Use a knife to release any air bubbles trapped in the jars and adjust the lids.

Place the jars on a rack in a canner with enough hot water to cover the jars by at least 1 inch. Bring the water to a boil and simmer for 30 minutes. (At altitudes of between 1 and 3 thousand feet, boil 35 minutes; between 3 and 6 thousand feet, boil 40 minutes; between 6 to 8 thousand feet, allow 45 minutes; and above 8 thousand feet, boil 50 minutes.) Remove the jars from the water and allow to cool. Check the seals after 30 minutes and again when the jars have cooled.

Makes 6 to 8 pints

Sweet Cucumber Pickles

When making pickles the old maxim is "twenty four-hours from vine to brine."

In her fine book, *Martha's Pioneer Cookbook, Wyoming Centennial Edition*, Martha Fehlman of Powell, Wyoming, gives some good general advice on making pickles (see Mail-Order Sources).

When choosing cucumbers select those that are light skinned, attractively warted, not more that two inches in diameter and young enough so that seeds have not matured. The cucumber should be as fresh as possible, best the same day picked.

Wash the cucumbers thoroughly under cold running water and use a soft vegetable brush to remove any soil. Clinging soil causes bacteria that is hard to destroy. Remove all blossom ends—they are a source of enzymes that are responsible for softening cucumbers during fermentation.

Use pure granulated NONIODIZED pickling salt, containing less than one percent anti-caking chemicals, usually labeled free flowing. Anti-caking chemical makes brine cloudy, iodized table salt may cause pickles to darken. Use a high grade cider or white distilled vinegar of 4 to 6 percent acidity.

The sweet pickle recipe that follows was given to me by my friend and neighbor Olive Breeden of the Box 3 Ranch near Carpenter, Wyoming. Olive makes the best sweet pickles I've ever tasted. They are wonderfully crisp and almost translucent. She credits her friend Vesta Pacheco, who used to own the grocery store in Carpenter, with the original recipe. The nine to ten pints of pickles this recipe makes may sound like a lot, but they disappear very quickly!

7 pounds small cucumbers	**2 teaspoons salt**
2 cups pickling lime (see Appendix)	**1 teaspoon mustard seed**
2 quarts apple cider vinegar	**1 teaspoon celery seed**
4½ pounds sugar	**1 teaspoon pickling spice**

Slice the cucumbers ¹/₄ inch thick. Mix lime and 2 gallons of water and soak the cucumbers in this solution for 24 hours. Using clean hands (lime makes cucumbers very crisp, so use your hands to prevent breaking them) stir cucumbers 2 or 3 times during the soaking.

Drain the lime water and rinse very thoroughly with cold running water. Cover the pickles with clear, cold water and soak for 3 hours.

Combine the vinegar, sugar, salt, mustard seed, celery seed, and pickling spice. Soak the pickles in this cold mixture overnight.

The next morning, in a large non-aluminum kettle or pot, boil the pickle mixture for 35 minutes, or until the pickles become translucent. Have sterilized canning jars and lids ready. Remove the pickles to the sterilized jars with a slotted spoon. Pour enough of the hot juices over the pickles to cover them, leaving $1/2$-inch headroom. Make sure no bubbles are in the jars by running a knife around the top to break the bubbles. Carefully wipe the lip of the jar with a clean, damp cloth and place the sterilized lid and screw tops on jars. Tighten the lids snugly but not hard. The jars should be properly sealed at this time, but as an added precaution process them in a boiling water bath.

Place the jars on a rack in a canner filled with enough hot water to cover them by 1 to 2 inches. Bring to a boil and simmer for 5 to 10 minutes. Remove from the water and allow to cool. After half an hour, check vacuum seal. If there is any overflow, rinse off the jar and screw top and wipe dry with a clean cloth. Place a new sterilized lid on the pickles and reprocess for 5 to 10 minutes as described above.

Makes 9 to 10 pints

Pickled Peaches

The Spanish brought peaches to the New World in the sixteenth century. This fruit thrived and quickly spread northward—both through cultivation and by a widespread escape from cultivation into the wild. Dried and canned peaches were special treats for pioneers moving west, and once settled, homesteaders established their own orchards.

In the early years, when many families lived in sod houses with few amenities, drying fruit and vegetables or packing them in brine were the most common methods of preservation. As life became marginally easier, pioneer women got out their old family recipes for jams, jellies, and conserves and started "putting up." Today, many ranch and farm women of my acquaintance carry on this tradition.

I found the recipe below for pickled peaches handwritten in an old cookbook that belonged to my grandmother. She had noted that it came from Mrs. Stevenson Scott and that "these peaches are delicious with ham, turkey, or roast pork."

3 pounds brown sugar

1 pound granulated sugar

1 quart distilled white vinegar

18 to 24 3-inch cinnamon sticks

1 bushel peaches, ripe, but unblemished

3/4 to 1 cup (2 to 3 ounces) whole cloves

In a large nonreactive saucepan, bring the sugars, vinegar, and cinnamon to a boil and simmer for 20 minutes.

Meanwhile, dip the peaches quickly in boiling water and slip off the skins. Stick 4 cloves into each peach. Cook one-fourth of the peaches at a time in the simmering syrup until tender but firm, 6 to 8 minutes. With a slotted spoon, transfer the peaches to wide-mouthed, sterilized jars. If desired, put a cinnamon stick in each jar for additional flavor and attractive presentation. Cover with syrup and seal. Process following the instructions on page 171.

Makes 18 to 24 quarts

Buster Childers' Sauerkraut Salad

Former rodeo bull rider Buster Childers and his wife, Sylvia McCoy Childers, are cattle ranchers along the Colorado-Wyoming border. Their ranch has been in Sylvia's family since 1928. Her grandfather Steve McCoy, an old-time cowboy, was a good hand with cattle and an able cook on roundups. Her grandmother Lottie was famous for her apple pies.

Buster is also a noted cook. His Sauerkraut Salad is unusual, sweet and sour, crisp and delicious. It can be made up to one week in advance if kept in the refrigerator.

1 ½ cups sauerkraut, juices reserved

1 cup sugar

½ cup cider vinegar

½ cup chopped red or yellow onion

½ cup chopped celery

¼ cup chopped pimientos or roasted red peppers

¼ cup chopped red bell pepper

¼ chopped green bell pepper

Rinse the sauerkraut in cold water and squeeze dry. In a nonreactive saucepan, combine the sauerkraut juice with the sugar and vinegar. Stirring constantly, bring to a boil. Allow to cool and combine with the sauerkraut, onion, celery, pimientos, and bell peppers. Refrigerate the salad until ready to serve.

Serves 6 to 8

Olive Breeden's Rhubarb Pie

Rhubarb, often called "pie plant," was a popular perennial in homestead gardens. If you look around the ruins of old homesteads in the early months of summer, you are likely to find a brave stand of crimson rhubarb, the last vestige of some early settlers' hard work, hopes, and dreams.

This recipe for a deliciously sweet and tart rhubarb pie was given to me by my friend Olive Breeden of the Box 3 Ranch near Carpenter, Wyoming.

Pie dough for a single-crust 9-inch pie

1 ½ cups sugar

¼ cup unbleached all-purpose flour

1 teaspoon ground cinnamon

2 large eggs, beaten

3 cups chopped rhubarb (½- to ¾-inch pieces)

Preheat the oven to 400° F.

Roll out the dough and line a 9-inch pie pan with the crust.

In a mixing bowl, combine the sugar, flour, and cinnamon. Whisk in the eggs. Add the rhubarb and mix until well combined. Pour the rhubarb mixture into the pie crust. Bake on the lower shelf of the oven for 15 minutes. Move the pie to the middle shelf of the oven and reduce the temperature to 350° F. Continue to bake for about 1 hour, or until the top of the pie is puffed and golden and a knife inserted in the center comes out clean.

Serves 6

Hattie Wilson's Apple Pie

Mrs. Everett Wilson, Hattie to her friends, does not make her famous apple pies—she builds them. Her method is unusual. She makes an incredibly light and flaky crust with boiling water. Unlike most apple pies, there is no space between the top crust and the apples in a Wilson pie because Hattie poaches the apple slices in sugar syrup before layering them in the crust. Ranchers tend to be self-sufficient both by necessity and inclination, and Hattie Wilson is a prime example of this spirit. A self-taught baker, she approached pie-making as she did other challenges in her life on the ranch, studying the task at hand and figuring out how to do it well.

BOILING WATER CRUST

1 cup vegetable shortening

2 teaspoons sugar

½ teaspoon salt

2½ cups unbleached all-purpose flour

APPLE FILLING

¾–1 cup sugar, depending on the tartness of
   the apples

Grated zest and juice of ½ lemon

5–6 large firm Jonathan or Granny Smith
   apples

1½–2 tablespoons instant or cracked tapioca

1 teaspoon ground cinnamon (optional)

Pinch of nutmeg

2 to 3 tablespoons butter

To make the pie crust, in a mixing bowl, beat together the shortening and ¹/₂ cup of boiling water until the mixture is light and fluffy. Add the sugar and salt and combine well. Add the flour and mix with a fork until the crust begins to come together. Do not overmix or the crust will be tough. Gather the dough into a ball and allow to rest a few minutes at room temperature while preparing the filling.

To make the pie filling, combine ¹/₄ cup of water, ¹/₂ cup of the sugar, and the lemon zest in a large saucepan. Bring to a boil, stirring, until the sugar is dissolved. If desired, pour the syrup through a strainer to remove the zest. Add the lemon juice and set the syrup aside.

Peel, core, and slice the apples about ¹/₄ inch thick. Add the apple slices to the hot syrup and simmer gently over medium-low heat for 3 to 4 minutes, until they are slightly softened but still hold their shape. With a slotted spoon, remove the apple slices from the syrup and place in a mixing bowl. Return the syrup to high heat and boil 1 to 2 minutes until it thickens slightly and is reduced to about ¹/₂ cup. Allow the syrup to cool slightly. Add the tapioca, cinnamon, and nutmeg to the apples and toss gently.

PAGES 176–77: *Colorado Peach Cobbler, Olaya's Cherry Pie, and Hattie Wilson's Apple Pie*

Divide the pie crust dough in half. Between sheets of lightly floured waxed paper, roll out the crust until $^1/_8$ to $^1/_4$ inch thick. Carefully remove the top sheet of paper and invert the crust into a 9-inch pie dish.

Fill the crust with the apple mixture. Sprinkle 2 to 4 tablespoons of the remaining sugar over the apples and dot with the butter.

Preheat the oven to 425° F.

Roll out the top crust. Gently fold the crust in half and place it on top of the pie filling. Carefully unfold it and trim the edges, making sure to leave enough to fold under the edge of the lower crust. Moisten the rim of the lower crust with a little water. Turn the edge of the top crust under the lower crust and pinch the rim in a running pinch design using the thumbs and forefingers of both hands, then press down at intervals with the tines of a fork. Using a small, sharp knife, cut your design—usually an "A" for apple—and 3 to 4 slashes in the top crust to allow steam to escape. Sprinkle a little extra sugar over the top crust.

Bake the pie on the bottom shelf of the oven. After 15 minutes, reduce the oven temperature to 350° F and continue to bake for 30 to 40 minutes, until the crust is golden brown and the apple filling is bubbling.

Makes 6 to 8 servings

Colorado Peach Cobbler

Colorado orchards produce delicious peaches. In late summer, when the peaches ripen on the western slope of the Rockies, our friend Jack Anderson gets in his pickup truck and heads for the mountains. He returns to his ranch in the plains with a full load of ripe, fragrant peaches, which he distributes to friends and neighbors for fifty miles around. Then begins a frenzy of baking, freezing, putting up, and just enjoying the last fruits of summer.

1½ pounds fresh peaches

¾ to 1 cup sugar, depending on the sweetness of fruit

½ teaspoon ground cinnamon

¼ teaspoon ground mace

1 cup unbleached all-purpose flour

1 teaspoon baking powder

¾ cup milk

2 large eggs, lightly beaten

6 tablespoons butter

Preheat the oven to 375° F.

Bring a saucepan full of water to a boil. Dip the peaches into the boiling water for 10 to 20 seconds, remove, and slip off the skins. Cut the peaches into wedges. In a mixing bowl, toss the peaches gently with ¼ cup of the sugar, the cinnamon, and the mace. In a separate mixing bowl, combine the flour, remaining sugar to taste, and the baking powder.

Stir in the milk and eggs until just blended.

Place the butter in 9-inch square baking pan and place it in the oven until the butter is melted and hot. Remove the pan from the oven and immediately pour the batter over the butter. Spoon the peach mixture evenly over the batter. Bake 40 to 45 minutes, until puffed and browned.

Serves 6

Helen Winger's Devil's Food Cake with Brown Sugar Frosting

Helen Raney Winger is known for her kind heart and her wonderful sour-cream devil's food cake.

Mrs. Winger was born into a homesteading family in Johnson, Kansas, in 1897. She doesn't remember where the recipe for this cake originated but recalls bartering eggs and cream for the cocoa she needed to make it during the Depression.

Helen and her husband, Clarence, raised cattle all their lives. Today the Winger Cattle Company is run by their grandchildren.

DEVIL'S FOOD CAKE

½ cup cocoa powder

2¼ cups all-purpose flour

2 cups sugar

1 cup sour cream

2 large eggs, beaten

2 teaspoons baking soda

1 teaspoon vanilla extract

⅛ teaspoon salt

BROWN SUGAR FROSTING

10 tablespoons firmly packed brown sugar

6 tablespoons melted butter

6 tablespoons light cream

½ cup shredded sweetened coconut

To make the cake, lightly grease and flour a 9-by-13-inch baking pan.

Place the cocoa in a saucepan. Pour 1 cup boiling water over the cocoa and whisk until smooth. Cook the cocoa mixture over medium heat, stirring constantly, for 2 to 3 minutes, until it thickens. Allow the mixture to cool.

Preheat the oven to 350° F.

In a large mixing bowl, combine the flour and sugar. Stir in the sour cream and eggs. Add the batter to the saucepan with the cooled cocoa mixture and stir to combine.

Add 3 tablespoons of water and the baking soda to the mixing bowl. Scrape any batter clinging to the side of the bowl and stir to combine it with the baking soda mixture. Add it along with the vanilla and salt to the batter in the saucepan and mix. Pour the batter into the prepared pan.

Bake 30 to 40 minutes, until a wooden pick inserted in the center of the cake comes out clean. Remove the cake from the oven and preheat the broiler. Frost the cake with Brown Sugar Frosting while still warm.

To make the frosting, combine the brown sugar, butter, and cream in a small saucepan. Place the pan over medium-high heat and bring almost to a boil. Stir in the coconut. Spread the frosting over the top of the warm cake. Place the cake under the broiler for 2 to 3 minutes, or until the frosting is brown and bubbly.

Serves 12

Chocolate Torte Cake

Mrs. Mae E. Michelson of the Michelson Ranch near Big Piney, Wyoming, often recounted how she came by a marvelous recipe for chocolate torte cake. When her friend Nellie Cushing was a young bride straight from the East, she often attended picnics in the town of Saratoga, Wyoming. There was a local woman who always brought a delicious cake but who would not give the recipe to anyone. Undaunted, Mrs. Cushing persisted. She finally bought the recipe for $50, then shared it with her friends. Nellie Cushing always maintained that the secret to this cake lay in mixing the butter and sugar by hand.

TORTE

2½ cups sifted cake flour

1 teaspoon baking soda

½ cup butter, softened

1 cup granulated sugar

1 cup firmly packed brown sugar

3 large eggs, separated

1½ cups milk

2 squares unsweetened baking chocolate, melted

1 teaspoon vanilla extract

ICING

½ cup butter, softened

2½ cups confectioners' sugar

2 ounces unsweetened baking chocolate, melted

½ teaspoon vanilla extract

Pinch of salt

2 to 3 tablespoons light cream

To make the cake, preheat the oven to 350° F. Lightly grease and flour three 9-inch round cake pans. Sift the flour and baking soda together 3 times.

In a large bowl, cream the butter and sugars by hand. In a medium bowl, beat the egg whites until stiff but not dry. In another bowl, beat the egg yolks until they turn pale yellow. Add the beaten egg yolks to the butter mixture and stir until blended. Stir in half of the dry ingredients alternately with the milk. Add the chocolate and half of the beaten egg whites. Stir in the remaining dry ingredients and milk. Fold in the remaining egg whites and vanilla extract and pour into the prepared pans.

Bake 25 minutes, until a wooden pick inserted in the center of the cake comes out clean. Cool the cakes in the pans 2 to 3 minutes Remove to wire racks to cool completely.

To make the icing, in a mixing bowl, combine the butter with the confectioners' sugar, chocolate, vanilla, and salt. Mix in enough cream to make a spreadable consistency, and fill and frost the cake.

Serves 6 to 8

Texas Apple Cake

The Noelke family has a long and interesting history as Texas ranchers. In 1840, two-year-old Ferdinand Noelke arrived in Corpus Christi as an orphan. His parents, part of a group of Germans who had purchased land in Texas, died from smallpox on the ship that was bringing them from Europe. The baby was adopted and raised by a Texas doctor and his wife. Because the child stood to inherit his parents' land, he was allowed to retain his name.

When the Civil War began, Ferdinand joined Terry's Texas Rangers and fought on the side of the Confederacy. After the war, the young man returned to Texas, claimed his birthright, and took up ranching. He married Alice Patterson Blackwell, formerly of Princeton, New Jersey, and started a family. By the late 1800s, the large influx of homesteaders into east Texas began to crowd out ranchers who grazed their cattle on the open range. The Noelkes sold their land and moved to the less-populated western part of the state. The rugged west Texas terrain suited the family, and today the sixth generation of Noelkes in Texas continues to ranch there.

The recipe for this wonderful old-fashioned apple cake was given to us by Ferdinand Noelke's great great-granddaughter, Gretchen Noelke. It was first published in a collection of family recipes compiled by Gretchen's first cousin Patricia Eckert to raise money for Heritage House, part of historic Fort Concho in San Angelo, Texas. The recipe itself comes from Patsy's mother-in-law, affectionately known as "Mamaw."

2¼ cups flour

½ teaspoon ground cloves

½ teaspoon ground cinnamon

½ teaspoon ground allspice

½ teaspoon ground nutmeg

⅔ cup butter, softened

2 cups sugar

3 large eggs

½ cup buttermilk

1 teaspoon baking soda

3 cups chopped peeled Golden Delicious apples

1 teaspoon vanilla extract

Preheat the oven to 350° F. Grease and flour a 9-by-13-inch baking pan.

Mix the flour with the cloves, cinnamon, allspice, and nutmeg.

In a mixing bowl, cream the butter and sugar. Add the eggs and beat well. Stir in the buttermilk with the baking soda. Stir in the dry ingredients. Stir in the apples and vanilla. Pour the batter into the prepared pan.

Bake for 30 to 40 minutes, until the cake is golden brown and a wooden pick inserted in the center comes out clean.

Serves 8 to 12

NOTE: If the apples are very juicy, add a little more flour.

Two Old-fashioned Taffies

Candy-making was a special treat for pioneer children, and taffy pulls were the best treat of all. When I was a child, my grandmother May Cox used to amuse us with stories about the Old West. Sometimes on a winter's afternoon we would have an old-fashioned taffy pull, just as the early settlers did. As a child, I loved both the making and the eating of the taffy. It's still fun to make, but as an adult I would advise others to consume it carefully!

My grandmother usually made molasses taffy, but vinegar taffy was another popular pioneer recipe. Most well-stocked pantries had a small bottle of precious vanilla extract that was used sparingly as a flavoring and dabbed behind ladies' ears as a fragrance. If there was vanilla to spare it was sometimes added to the vinegar taffy, which then became vanilla taffy.

Grandma's Molasses Taffy

1 ¼ cups dark molasses

¾ cup sugar

1 tablespoon cider vinegar

¼ teaspoon cream of tartar

2 tablespoons butter, cut into pieces

⅛ teaspoon baking soda

⅛ teaspoon salt

Lightly butter a jelly-roll pan or baking sheet. Combine the molasses, sugar, and vinegar in a heavy 3-quart saucepan. Cook over medium-low heat, stirring, until the sugar is dissolved and the syrup comes to a boil. Stir in the cream of tartar. Cover and let boil for 2 to 3 minutes. Uncover and wash down the sides of the pan with a pastry brush dipped in cold water. Insert a candy thermometer into the syrup. Without stirring, continue to boil over medium heat to just below the firm ball stage, 240° F. Remove from the heat and gradually stir in the butter. Add the baking soda and salt. Stir enough to blend, then return to the heat and continue to boil gently until the mixture reaches the hard ball stage, 260° F (a few drops of syrup drizzled into a bowl of cold water will hold a very firm shape). Tilting the pan away from you, carefully pour the hot candy onto the prepared pan.

When cool enough to handle, gather the taffy into a ball with buttered or oiled hands. Pull the taffy out about 12 inches and fold it back upon itself with a twist. (This can be done with a partner. Each person takes one end of the taffy.) Keep pulling, folding, and twisting, until the candy lightens in color and begins to harden. Pull it into a long rope and cut it into 1- to 2-inch lengths with buttered kitchen scissors. If desired, wrap each piece of taffy in waxed paper. Store the taffy in an airtight container in a cool, dry place so it doesn't get sticky.

Makes about 1 pound

Vanilla Taffy

2½ cups sugar

2 tablespoons cider vinegar

1 tablespoon butter

1 teaspoon vanilla extract

Lightly butter a jelly-roll pan or baking sheet. In a saucepan, combine the sugar, ½ cup of water, the vinegar, and the butter. Stir together over medium-low heat until the sugar is dissolved. Insert a candy thermometer into the syrup. Without stirring, continue to boil, over medium heat, until the syrup reaches the hard ball stage, 260° F. Stir in the vanilla. Tilting the pan away from you, carefully pour the candy onto the prepared pan.

When cool enough to handle, gather the taffy into a ball with buttered or oiled hands. Pull, cut, and store the taffy as described in the recipe for Molasses Taffy.

Makes about 1 pound

Penuche

This old-fashioned candy was a favorite of pioneer children.

2 cups firmly packed brown sugar

1 cup heavy whipping cream

1 tablespoon butter

½ cup chopped English walnuts

Lightly butter an 8- to 10-inch platter or pyrex dish. In a large, heavy saucepan, combine the sugar, cream, and butter. Bring to a boil and insert a candy thermometer into the syrup. Cook over medium-low heat until the mixture reaches the firm ball stage when a small amount of syrup is dropped in a cup of cold water. Remove from the heat and stir in the walnuts.

Beat the candy with a wooden spoon until it becomes creamy. Pour onto the prepared pan and allow to cool. Mark squares on the surface of the candy with a knife before it cools completely.

Makes about 1 pound

Mary Anderson's Lemon Pudding

Mary Anderson is remembered as a patient, soft-spoken woman who loved to cook and entertain. Like other ranch women of her era, Mrs. Anderson was busy from before dawn until well into the night. By modern standards, ranch life in 1935 was rough. When Earl and Mary Anderson moved to their ranch near Grover, Colorado, there was no electricity in the house and no indoor plumbing. Water for cooking, washing, and bathing had to be carried in from the well and heated on a wood-burning stove. Besides caring for her own family, Mrs. Anderson cooked, washed, and ironed for the ranch cowboys, raised chickens, and cultivated a large garden. Friends and neighbors felt free to drop by for dinner because Mary always prepared for extras. She baked twice a week and made wonderful hot rolls for company on Sundays. Her daughter Peggy Adams doesn't remember her mother ever complaining: "She did what needed to be done and did it well." This is her recipe for lemon pudding.

¾ cup sugar

2 tablespoons unbleached all-purpose flour

1 tablespoon butter, softened

2 large eggs, separated

1 cup milk

1 large lemon, zested (about 1 ½ teaspoons) and juiced (about 3 tablespoons)

Confectioners' sugar (optional)

Preheat the oven to 325° F.

In a mixing bowl, cream the sugar, flour, and butter. Beat the egg yolks and add the milk, zest, and lemon juice. Gradually add the yolk mixture to the sugar mixture, stirring constantly.

In a clean bowl, beat the egg whites until stiff but not dry. Fold into the lemon mixture. Carefully pour the mixture into an 8-inch square baking pan or 3-cup casserole. Place the pan in a larger pan filled with hot water. Bake for 1 hour, until it is set. The pudding can be served warm or cold. If desired, dust with confectioners' sugar before serving.

Serves 4 to 6

DUDE RANCHES

A WESTERN HERITAGE

*E*VEN BEFORE THE NINETEENTH CENTURY ENDED, Easterners were going west to see the rapidly disappearing Wild West. Writers of books and articles and traveling Wild-West shows portrayed the West as bigger than life, and they especially glorified the American cowboy. Thus it was only natural that many people wanted to experience the West at first hand, and where could they better do so than on a ranch.

The first western dude ranch was born during the last years of the long trail drives and at the time when large ranches were being established on the northern plains. The year was 1882. Bert Rumsey of Buffalo, New York, visited a ranch located near today's Medora, North Dakota. This horse ranch was owned by the Eaton brothers—Howard, Alden, and Willis—who had come west from their native Pennsylvania to settle in 1879. They called their ranch Custer Trail because General George Custer had once camped nearby. Bert Rumsey was so pleased with ranch life that he remained longer than he had planned and he soon insisted on paying for his keep. Reluctant at first, the Eatons finally agreed to take his money, and the dude ranch business was born. The Eatons were the first to apply the term "dude" to these eastern visitors who paid twenty-five dollars a month to stay on their ranch and eat bacon or sowbelly, beans, potatoes, and wild game. It appears that the Eatons used the word to mean a "dandy," or "sport," or "outsider," but the word began to take on a new meaning in the West, that of a city person, or tenderfoot, or visitor. Since the word "dude" applied to males, someone later coined the word "dudeen" to apply to females, but it never came into wide usage.

At the Eatons' many of the paying guests helped with the cattle and other ranch work. Accommodations were rather primitive, with the visitors staying in sod-roofed log cabins or in tents. The Eatons' business continued to grow until the winter of 1886–87, when vicious winter storms swept the plains, killing thousands of cattle and nearly all of the Eatons' horses. That same winter their ranch house burned to the ground. But other "dude" ranches had come into operation, a few being called "guest" ranches. By 1900, dozens of such ranches could be found across the West. By 1904, the Eatons were operating their dude ranch under the shadow of the Big Horn Mountains near Sheridan, Wyoming. Movie stars as Fred MacMurray, Cary Grant, and Carol Baker, among others, spent time on the seven-thousand-acre Eaton Dude Ranch, adjoining the Big Horn National Forest. The ranch continues to operate today, managed by the fourth generation of the family.

By the early decades of the twentieth century, the number of dude ranches in the west increased considerably, as more and more city folks and Easterners were willing to pay to experience a way of life that was once available only to the hardy. Dude ranching became so popular that owners organized their own national association. In 1936, Lawrence B. "Lon" Smith, something of a connoisseur of dude-ranch life, set down in his book *Dude Ranches and Ponies* thirty-six rules for dudes and dudeens to follow. They included:

DON'T fail to acquaint yourself, as soon as you can, with the customs of the ranch, the meal hours and such. It will make things easier for yourself and everyone else.

DON'T grumble about things; if you have a kick, go to he boss and register it, and if it is a fair one, he will fix you up or tell you why it can't be done.

DON'T arrive with several trunks of fancy clothes and a litter of hand baggage with the idea of staggering the inhabitants and the other guests. Wear comfortable but serviceable clothes; they look better and you will have more fun.

DON'T be late to meals; remember the cook has *some* job and usually cooks for two outfits—the savages [ranch hands] and the dudes—and by the time one meal is over it is time to start getting the next.

DON'T lie in bed mornings and then expect to get a ham omelet when you get to the grub-pile. If you are not well you will be taken care of, but don't get in the habit.

DON'T try to dress like a buckaroo [term for cowboy in the Pacific Northwest] and carry a lot of things you don't know how to use. You may be called on to give an exhibition some day and it may be embarrassing.

DON'T be a stiff shirt; join in the fun and do your bit with the talents you possess.

DON'T be unreasonable or a crank; just be a good sport; use a little judgment and be a bit considerate, and you will be *"settin' pretty all the way."*

For people weary of urban life, the dude ranch has become the place to gaze over the mighty western landscape, to sleep under the Western stars—or perhaps in a frontier-style log cabin—and to breathe deeply the strong but soothing air of the plains and mountains. Visitors take horseback rides, help with ranch chores, or simply relax and imagine what life must have been like in the Old West—if only for a brief period of time. Of course, they also enjoy hearty ranch cuisine. While the Eatons and other early dude ranches once served nothing but the conventional old-time menu—beans; bacon; tomatoes; tough, freshly killed beef; sourdough bread; coffee; dried apples; and the occasional potato—there is far more variety in the fare served today. Dude ranch food is simply better, and some dude or guest ranches serve meals of the same quality as those served by the best Western restaurants.

—DAVID DARY

Eatons' Ranch Oatcakes

Eatons' Ranch, the oldest of all western dude ranches, is located at the base of Wyoming's Big Horn Mountains. It offers spectacular scenery and 7,000 acres to ride on, and it is one of the few ranches that allows guests who are competent horsemen to ride without being accompanied by a wrangler.

When Nancy Ferguson from Eatons' Ranch gave me their recipe for oatmeal pancakes, I feared that they would be hearty but heavy. I couldn't have been more wrong—these are some of the best pancakes we have ever eaten! They are light and have an interesting texture and wonderful flavor.

2 cups rolled oats

2 cups buttermilk

½ cup unbleached all-purpose flour

1 teaspoon salt

1 teaspoon baking soda

3 large eggs, beaten

2 tablespoons sugar

**¼ cup melted vegetable shortening or butter
   (Do not substitute oil for shortening)**

Combine the oats and buttermilk in a mixing bowl. Cover and refrigerate overnight.

Sift together the flour, salt, and baking soda. Add the flour mixture, eggs, sugar, and shortening to the oatmeal mixture and stir well.

Drop by large spoonfuls onto a hot, lightly oiled griddle. Cook until bubbles form on the surface. Turn and cook until golden brown on the other side. Serve the pancakes with syrup, jam, or honey.

Makes 24 to 30 (3-inch) pancakes

Circle Z Ranch "Best Bread in the World"

Nestled in the foothills of the remote and romantic Santa Rita Mountains lies the Circle Z, the oldest continuously operating guest ranch in southern Arizona. The ranch was started in 1926 by Lee and Helen Zinsmeister. The Zinsmeisters envisioned the Circle Z as a place where guests, accustomed to good service, could enjoy the pleasures of life on a big cattle ranch. To assure that everyone would be congenial, the ranch required prospective guests to provide references during its early years.

The current owner, Lucia Nash, vacationed at the Circle Z as a child. In 1974, when she heard that the ranch and adjacent lands were going to be developed, Mrs. Nash stepped in and bought it. She has increased the original 800-acre ranch to 6,000 acres, preserving both the land and the Circle Z tradition.

Life at the Circle Z centers around the massive adobe lodge that was once the Zinsmeisters' house. Guests stay in adobe cottages scattered around the ranch compound. Riding is the main activity on the Circle Z, which prides itself on its gentle, well-bred quarter horses, most of which are born, raised, and trained on the ranch.

The ranch dining room serves a variety of well-prepared dishes. On Fridays, Pancho Cordova, who has worked at the Circle Z for more than twenty years, cooks Mexican food all day long. Guests have been known to change travel plans to arrive in time to breakfast on Pancho's *huevos rancheros*. Another Circle Z favorite is the whole-wheat–oatmeal bread that guests have dubbed "The Best Bread in the World."

1 cup rolled oats

1 tablespoon salt

½ cup honey

2 tablespoons butter, melted

3 (¼-ounce) packages active dry yeast

2½ cups unbleached all-purpose flour or bread flour

2½ cups whole wheat flour

1 large egg yolk, lightly beaten

Sesame seeds

Place the oats in a large mixing bowl and pour in 2 cups of boiling water. Stir in the salt, honey, and butter and set aside to cool until the mixture is lukewarm.

Meanwhile, dissolve the yeast in ⅓ cup of lukewarm water. Add the yeast to the cooled oat mixture and stir well. Gradually stir in the flours. On a lightly floured surface, knead the dough for about 10 minutes, until elastic. Return the dough to the bowl and cover loosely with a clean kitchen towel and set aside to rise in a warm, draft-free place for 1 hour. Divide the dough in half, knead briefly, and shape into 2 loaves. Place each loaf in a buttered 8½-by-4½-inch loaf pan and allow to rise until the dough is barely over the top of the pan.

Preheat the oven to 350° F.

Brush the loaves with the beaten egg yolk and sprinkle with sesame seeds. Bake on the middle shelf of the oven for 35 to 40 minutes, until golden brown.

Makes 2 loaves

Skyline Ranch Baby Back Ribs with Chipotle Barbecue Sauce

Skyline Guest Ranch is located near Telluride in one of the most beautiful settings in south-western Colorado. The ranch started as a logging camp in the early 1900s. It was purchased in 1968 by Dave and Sherry Farney, who ran a summer mountaineering school there until 1983, when it became a guest ranch. To preserve the property, the Farneys have deeded future development rights to the Nature Conservancy.

In summer, horseback riding is the major activity at the ranch. Riders learn to establish a relationship with their mounts by studying herd behavior and learning to "think like a horse." During the summer, overnight horseback trips are arranged each week. There are also spring and fall four-day pack trips. Skyline caters to families but doesn't have a special children's program.

During the summer, the dining room is only for ranch guests. During the winter months, however, it is open to the public. The food at Skyline has a well-deserved reputation for being interesting and good. Former chef Gary Thut, whose recipes follow, has moved on to open a restaurant in a restored theater in the nearby town of Rico. His place at the Skyline Ranch has been filled by another talented chef, Joe Cobb, who is a specialist in cowboy Dutch-oven cooking.

2 tablespoons coarsely ground black pepper

2 tablespoons seasoning salt

2 tablespoons mild chili powder

1 ½ teaspoons minced dried garlic

½ teaspoon cayenne pepper

4 slabs pork baby back ribs (about 1 ½ pounds each), left whole but cracked between ribs, or 6 pounds beef ribs

3 cups Chipotle Barbecue Sauce (recipe follows)

In a small bowl, combine the pepper, seasoning salt, chili powder, garlic, and cayenne. Rub the ribs generously on both sides with this seasoning mixture. Place in a single layer of ribs on a wire rack in a shallow roasting pan. Cut the rib racks into 3 to 4 sections if your pan is not large enough for the whole slabs. Cover tightly with aluminum foil and place on the middle rack in the oven. Turn on the oven to 250° F and cook the ribs for 3 to 3 ½ hours, until tender. Remove the foil during the last 10 minutes of cooking. At this point the ribs can be refrigerated, wrapped in foil, for up to 24 hours.

When ready to finish the ribs, prepare charcoal for grilling, placing the grill rack 6 inches above the coals. When the coals are white-hot, brush the ribs on both sides with the barbecue sauce. Arrange the ribs on the hot grill rack. Cover and cook 15 to 20 minutes, until the ribs are lightly charred and well glazed, turning and basting with the sauce 2 to 3 times. Serve the ribs with additional warm sauce, cole slaw, and Sweet Green Chile Cornbread (see page 197).

Makes 6 to 8 servings

Chipotle Barbecue Sauce

1 (28-ounce) can crushed tomatoes

¾ cup molasses

1 small onion, peeled and chopped (about ½
   cup)

¼ cup dry sherry or orange juice

1 tablespoon Worcestershire sauce

1 to 2 tablespoons chipotle chiles in adobo
   sauce (see Note)

1 clove garlic, peeled and crushed

1 teaspoon ground allspice

Salt and freshly ground black pepper

In a 3-quart saucepan, combine the tomatoes, molasses, onion, sherry, Worcestershire sauce, chipotles, garlic, allspice, and salt and pepper to taste. Bring to a simmer over medium-high heat. Reduce the heat to low and cook, uncovered, stirring occasionally, for 30 minutes. Remove from the heat and puree the mixture in a food processor. Return to low heat and simmer, stirring frequently, for an additional 45 minutes or until the sauce is reduced to about 1 quart.

Makes 1 quart

NOTE: Canned or jarred chipotles in adobo sauce can be found in specialty food stores or Latino markets. If not available, substitute 1 tablespoon bottled chili sauce or ketchup blended with $1/2$ teaspoon hot red pepper sauce and 1 or 2 drops of liquid smoke.

Skyline Ranch Sweet Green Chile Corn Bread

1 cup milk

1 tablespoon lemon juice

½ cup butter or margarine, melted

1 (4-ounce) can diced mild green chiles

2 large eggs

1 ½ cups cornmeal

¾ cup unbleached all-purpose flour

½ cup sugar

1 ¼ teaspoons baking soda

½ teaspoon salt

Preheat the oven to 375° F.

Butter a 9-inch square baking dish.

In a measuring cup, combine the milk and lemon juice. Let stand for 2 minutes. In a large mixing bowl, using an electric mixer at low speed, combine the melted butter, milk mixture, chiles, and eggs.

In a separate bowl, combine the cornmeal, flour, sugar, baking soda, and salt. Slowly beat the cornmeal mixture into the milk mixture at slow to medium speed. Blend until well combined. Pour the batter into the prepared baking dish. Bake for 20 to 30 minutes, or until a wooden pick inserted in the middle of the bread comes out clean. Cut the bread into squares and serve warm or at room temperature.

Makes 6 to 8 servings

West Pawnee Ranch Chicken-Fried Steak with Smothered Green Beans

The West Pawnee Ranch is located in northeastern Colorado, just south of the Wyoming border. This family-run working ranch offers guests the opportunity to try their hands at ranch chores such as moving cattle, branding, and calving. Roping lessons may also be arranged. The ranch is surrounded by the Pawnee National Grasslands, one of the best bird-watching locations in the United States.

Owners Paul and Luanne Timm serve old-fashioned country food. Chicken-fried steak with cream gravy, mashed potatoes, and smothered green beans are West Pawnee Ranch favorites.

½ cup unbleached all-purpose flour

Salt and ground black pepper

4 to 6 tenderized steaks

1 large egg, lightly beaten with 2 tablespoons
   water

¾ cup Bisquick or other buttermilk baking mix

3 tablespoons vegetable oil

Trail Drive and Bunkhouse Milk Gravy (see
   page 75)

Combine the flour with salt and pepper to taste. Dredge the steaks in the seasoned flour, dip in the egg mixture and coat with the Bisquick.

Heat the oil in a large, nonstick skillet over medium-high heat. Fry the steaks over medium heat for 4 to 5 minutes per side, turning once, until golden brown and cooked through. Remove the steaks to a serving platter and keep warm.

Use the drippings in the pan to make the milk gravy. Serve the steaks with the gravy.

Serves 4 to 6

Smothered Green Beans

1 pound fresh or frozen green beans

4 strips bacon

½ cup chopped onion

Salt and ground black pepper

Clean and snap the ends off the beans.

In a large, deep skillet, fry the bacon until it begins to crisp. Remove the bacon, chop, and reserve. Remove all but 1 tablespoon of the bacon drippings. Add the onion to the pan and sauté for 1 to 2 minutes, until translucent. Add the reserved bacon, ¼ cup of water, and the beans to the pan. Season to taste with salt and pepper. Cover and steam the beans 6 to 8 minutes, stirring once or twice, until tender-crisp.

Serves 4 to 6

The Lazy K Bar Ranch was founded in 1880 by Paul Van Cleve, who came west from Minnesota to settle the affairs of a cousin who had died with Custer at Little Big Horn. He loved Montana and decided to stay and take up ranching. Among the local characters who visited the Van Cleve ranch at Porcupine Butte were Calamity Jane, "Liver Eating" Johnson, and the Crow Chief Plenty Coups.

The Van Cleves had a large ranch house and during the summer months it was filled with visitors from the East. In 1922, they followed the examples of Teddy Roosevelt and the Eaton brothers and began to charge the "dudes" for room and board. The family built log cabins for their guests and, in the 1940s, put in a swimming pool. Modern plumbing has been installed in the cabins over the years, but the ranch maintains its original Old West flavor.

The Van Cleves are a multitalented and hospitable family. Barbara Van Cleve, widow of Western author Spike Van Cleve, owns and operates the Lazy K Bar with her son "Tack" (Paul) Van Cleve and her daughters Barbara and Carol. Mrs. Van Cleve has spent more than sixty years on the ranch and is the "hub" of the operation. Tack, a wonderful host, keeps the ranch running smoothly. Daughter Barbara's book, *Hard Twist: Western Ranch Women*, was published in 1995 to great acclaim. Carol is in charge of the ranch kitchen and of the horses and riding program. She is a lifetime member of ISSO (the International Side-Saddle Organization) and sometimes gives side-saddle clinics at the ranch.

Argentine stew is a Lazy K Bar Ranch favorite that was often prepared by Spike Van Cleve. The recipe for the wonderfully rich pound cake served at the ranch was given to the Van Cleve family many years ago by Mrs. Bateman of the Bateman Ranch in Texas.

Spike's Lazy K Bar Ranch Argentine Stew

2 pounds beef short ribs

5 slices bacon, diced

2 to 3 pound chicken, cut into serving pieces

2 cups cooked black-eyed peas, drained

4 Spanish, Italian, or Polish sausages (about 1½ pounds), cut into 2-inch pieces

1 medium head cabbage, thickly sliced

6 onions, peeled and quartered

1 small butternut or other winter squash, peeled and diced

2 garlic cloves, peeled and minced

1½ teaspoons salt

¼ teaspoon coarsely ground black pepper

Preheat the oven to 300° F.

Place the ribs, bacon, chicken, and black-eyed peas in a large Dutch oven with 6 cups of water. Cook in the oven for 1½ hours. Add the sausages and cabbage and cook for 20 minutes. Add the onions, squash, garlic, salt, and pepper and cook for 30 minutes more. If necessary, add more water during the cooking.

Serves 10 to 12

Bateman Pound Cake

3 cups sugar

1½ cups butter, softened

10 large eggs, separated

3 cups unbleached all-purpose flour

Preheat the oven to 325° F.

Grease two 9½-by-5½-inch loaf pans and line with parchment paper or waxed paper.

In a large mixing bowl, cream the sugar and butter well, about 15 minutes. Add the egg yolks and beat until well blended. In another large mixing bowl, beat the egg whites until they form soft peaks. One-fourth at a time, blend the whites and the flour alternately into the butter mixture. Mix well after each addition. Divide the batter between the prepared pans.

Bake for 1 to 1¼ hours, until the center is set and a wooden pick inserted in the middle of the cake comes out clean. Place on a wire rack to cool for 5 minutes. Invert the cakes and remove and discard the paper. Place the cakes on the rack to cool completely.

Makes 2 cakes

Teton Ridge's Four-Corners Grilled Chicken

Teton Ridge is a small, intimate guest ranch that caters primarily to adults. The ranch sits on a rise on the Idaho side of the Tetons. Guests have a choice of several on-site activities. The ranch staff will also arrange all-day trips to nearby Yellowstone Park with a knowledgeable naturalist, and whitewater rafting expeditions near Jackson.

The spectacular 10,000-square-foot lodge is constructed of mammoth lodgepole logs. It houses guests in five suites and has an impressive lounge with a cathedral ceiling and a magnificent view of the Grand Tetons.

Food at Teton Ridge is interesting, plentiful, and good. Marinated grilled chicken with a mild salsa is a summer specialty and in winter guests are crazy about the chef's delicious homemade gingersnaps.

1 (15-ounce) can tomatoes, drained and coarsely chopped

1 large onion, peeled and cubed

1 small red bell pepper, seeded and quartered

4 garlic cloves, peeled

½ cup fresh cilantro leaves

½ cup soy sauce

¼ cup canola oil or vegetable oil

Juice of 2 limes

Freshly ground black pepper

4 whole chicken breasts, split (8 breast halves)

Cilantro sprigs, for garnish

Place the tomatoes, onion, bell pepper, garlic, cilantro, soy sauce, oil, lime juice, and black pepper in a food processor and pulse on and off until all the vegetables are finely chopped.

Place the chicken in a large resealable plastic bag. Pour half of the tomato salsa over the chicken. Seal the bag and turn to coat the chicken with the seasonings. Reserve the remaining salsa to serve with the cooked chicken. Marinate the chicken in the refrigerator overnight.

Prepare charcoal for grilling, placing the rack about 6 inches above the coals. Remove the chicken from the marinade and grill over medium coals for about 30 minutes, until browned and cooked through. Turn often during grilling and baste the chicken with the marinade during the first 20 minutes. Serve the chicken with the reserved salsa, garnished with sprigs of cilantro.

Serves 6 to 8

Teton Ridge Gingersnaps

¾ cup vegetable shortening or butter, melted

1 cup sugar, plus additional for rolling

½ cup molasses

1 large egg

1 cup unbleached all-purpose flour

2 teaspoons baking soda

½ teaspoon ground cloves

½ teaspoon ground ginger

½ teaspoon ground cinnamon

½ teaspoon salt

In a mixing bowl, combine the shortening, sugar, molasses, and egg. Beat until creamy. Sift together the flour, baking soda, cloves, ginger, cinnamon, and salt. Add to the creamed mixture and blend well. Cover and chill the dough for 2 hours or overnight.

Preheat oven to 375° F.

Form the dough into pecan-size balls and roll in sugar. Place on a baking sheet and bake for 8 to 10 minutes, until they have spread and are lightly browned on the bottom. Remove from the oven and let cool for 1 to 2 minutes, then transfer the cookies to a wire rack to cool completely.

Makes 4 dozen

Home Ranch Marinated Grilled Vegetables with Smoky Tomato Vinaigrette

Located in the Elk River Valley at the edge of the Routt National Forest, the Home Ranch, a member of the Relais & Chateaux group, is known for its delicious and imaginative food and combination of European charm and cowboy culture. The ranch offers horseback riding, guided wilderness hikes, fly-fishing, an outdoor heated pool, and a strong children's program.

Many thanks to Clyde Nelson of the Home Ranch for sharing some of their recipes with us.

MARINADE

1 cup olive oil

¼ cup fresh basil leaves

3 to 4 sprigs fresh parsley

1 shallot, peeled

1 large garlic clove, peeled

2 leaves fresh sage

1 tablespoon lemon juice

1½ teaspoons grated Parmesan cheese

1½ teaspoons piñon (pine) nuts

Salt and ground black pepper

VEGETABLES

2 Japanese eggplants, halved lengthwise

2 red bell peppers, seeded and cut into thirds

1 small jicama, peeled and sliced ¼ inch thick

1 bunch scallions

8 stalks asparagus, trimmed

Hot crusty French bread

Smoky Tomato Vinaigrette (recipe follows)

To make the marinade, combine all the ingredients in a food processor or blender. Process until pureed.

Place the vegetables in a shallow baking pan and drizzle with enough of the marinade to coat them lightly. Marinate at room temperature for 1 hour.

Meanwhile, prepare charcoal for grilling, placing the grill rack about 6 inches above the coals. Grill the vegetables for 10 to 15 minutes, turning occasionally and basting with the marinade until they are lightly browned and tender. Reserve any remaining marinade to use as a dipping oil for hot crusty French bread. Serve with Smoky Tomato Vinaigrette.

Serves 12

Smoky Tomato Vinaigrette

2 to 4 Roma tomatoes

2 tablespoons fresh chopped basil

2 tablespoons fresh chopped marjoram

2 tablespoons fresh chopped tarragon

2 tablespoons fresh chopped thyme

2 tablespoons fresh chopped fennel

2 tablespoons lemon juice or wine vinegar

1 large shallot, peeled and coarsely chopped

½ cup extra-virgin olive oil

Grill or smoke the tomatoes until the skin begins to cook. Peel off the skin, cut the tomatoes crosswise, and squeeze out the seeds. Dice the tomatoes and place in a sieve to drain for a few minutes.

In a small bowl, combine the tomatoes and the basil, marjoram, tarragon, thyme, and fennel. Add the lemon juice and shallot. Gradually whisk in the olive oil.

Makes about 1 cup

Home Ranch Country Fried Rainbow Trout with Jalapeño Tartar Sauce

6 whole trout (½ to ¾ pound each) or 12 skinless trout fillets (3 to 4 ounces each)

1 large egg

1 cup buttermilk

½ cup self-rising flour

¼ teaspoon salt

Freshly ground black pepper

Pinch of cayenne pepper

1 ½ cups cornmeal

Peanut oil or vegetable oil, for frying

Small bunch parsley sprigs and lemon wedges, for garnish

Jalapeño Tartar Sauce (recipe follows)

Preheat the oven to 200° F.

Pat the fish dry with paper towels. In a shallow bowl, beat the egg and whisk in the buttermilk. In another shallow bowl combine the flour, salt, pepper, and cayenne. Place the cornmeal in another bowl. Dip the fish in the egg mixture, then the flour, and finally in the cornmeal.

Pour about 1 inch of oil into a large cast-iron skillet and heat to approximately 350° F. (The oil is ready for frying when a cube of bread dropped in turns golden brown in 1 minute.) Add 2 to 3 of the whole fish (or 4 to 5 of the fish fillets) to the pan and fry for 5 to 6 minutes on each side (3 to 4 minutes per side for the fillets). Remove and drain on paper towels. Keep warm in the oven while frying the remaining fish.

Drop well-dried parsley sprigs into the hot oil and fry until crisp. Remove and drain. Place the fish on a warm serving platter and garnish with the lemon and parsley.

Serves 6

Jalapeño Tartar Sauce

2 small scallions, minced (about 1 ½ tablespoons)

1 cup mayonnaise (preferably homemade)

1 tablespoon minced fresh parsley

1 teaspoon lemon or lime juice

½ teaspoon finely minced fresh dill or 1 tablespoon minced dill pickles

½ teaspoon capers, minced

1 hard-cooked large egg, chopped

½ to 1 fresh jalapeño chile, minced

In a small bowl, stir the scallions, mayonnaise, parsley, lemon juice, dill, capers, egg, and jalapeño to taste. Serve with fried fish.

Makes about 1 ¼ cups

Home Ranch Grilled Beef Tenderloin

3 tablespoons vegetable oil

1 whole beef tenderloin (4 to 5 pounds)

DRY RUB

3 tablespoons kosher salt

3 tablespoons coarsely ground black pepper

2 tablespoons minced garlic

1 tablespoon paprika

2 teaspoons minced bay leaf

1 ½ teaspoons cayenne pepper

1 ½ teaspoons dry mustard

¼ cup chopped fresh parsley

BARBECUE MOP

1 cup beef broth

¼ cup red wine

¼ cup Worcestershire sauce

2 tablespoons canola oil

2 serrano or jalapeño chiles, crushed

3 tablespoons bottled barbecue sauce

Salt and ground black pepper

Oil your hands and rub over the beef.

To make the dry rub, combine the salt and pepper, garlic, paprika, bay leaf, cayenne, mustard, and parsley in a small bowl. Rub this mixture over the beef. Allow to sit for 20 to 30 minutes.

Meanwhile, prepare charcoal for grilling, arranging a thicker layer of coals at one end for a hotter fire. Place the grill about 6 inches above coals.

To make the mopping sauce, combine the beef broth, the wine, the Worcestershire sauce, the oil, the chiles, the barbecue sauce and the salt and pepper in a small bowl. Place the tenderloin over white-hot coals and sear on one side for 5 minutes.

Brush with the mopping sauce, turn the roast 90 degrees to make criss-cross grill marks and grill another 5 minutes. Turn the roast over and grill another 5 minutes, continuing to mop every 5 minutes. Turn 2 more times to sear all the sides. Move the roast to a cooler part of the grill. Check the internal temperature with an instant-read thermometer. When it reaches 120° F move the meat to the coolest part of the grill and cover loosely with aluminum foil. Allow to rest for 10 to 15 minutes. The temperature should then be 124° F to 130° F. For medium-rare cook until 135° F.

Serves 10 to 12

Quilchena Cattle Company Rum Ribs

In 1857, the Guichon brothers arrived in California after a long and arduous journey from France. They immediately headed north to the gold fields of the Cariboo. The gold rush was on, but the brothers quickly concluded that there was more chance of becoming rich by supplying the other fortune seekers with food and equipment than by prospecting themselves.

The Guichon's supply and pack-train outfit prospered and they invested their profits in cattle. By 1890, the Guichon Cattle Company was the largest stock operation in the area, with some 2,000 head of cattle.

The family continued to purchase land and cattle and, in 1904, they acquired the property around Nicola Lake on which the current headquarters and hotel stand. Seeing opportunities for tourism in this beautiful area, they built a hotel in 1908. In the tongue of the local Salish people, "Quilchena" means "place where the willows grow," and that became the name of the ranch and new hotel.

Up until 1917, when it was closed due to Prohibition, Quilchena was the sight of interesting events and festive parties. Bill Minor, the train robber known as "the Grey Fox," was apprehended nearby and held at the hotel until he could be taken off to prison. Polo teams from Europe visited the ranch and exciting matches were held between the visitors and the locals, both Salish and Canadian. People came from near and far to dine in the hotel's fine restaurant and to experience life on one of Canada's greatest ranches.

In 1957, Quilchena was divided between two grandsons of the founders, Gerard Guichon and Guy Rose, once Guy and his family re-opened the Quilchena Hotel.

Visiting Quilchena is like stepping back into history. The hotel retains its original decor and charm. There are endless activities, including horseback riding, hiking, swimming, windsurfing, and fishing. The hotel's dining room and the saloon—with bullet holes in the bar—are popular destinations. Both are open to the public as well as to ranch guests, but it is important to reserve ahead because there are only nine tables in the restaurant.

This recipe is a favorite of both the Rose family and ranch guests. These ribs are easy to prepare and they taste great!

4 racks baby back ribs (about 6 pounds)

1 teaspoon seasoning salt

Glaze

1 cup brown sugar

½ cup chili sauce

¼ cup ketchup

¼ cup soy sauce

¼ cup dark rum

1 tablespoon dry mustard

¼ teaspoon ground pepper

Preheat the oven to 375° F.

Place the ribs in a roasting pan and sprinkle both sides with seasoning salt. Add 2 cups of water and cover with aluminum foil. Bake for approximately one hour, or until tender. Cut into pieces if desired.

Raise the oven temperature to 400° F. Make the glaze by mixing together the sugar, chili sauce, ketchup, soy sauce, rum, mustard, and pepper. Baste the ribs with glaze. Return to the oven for about 15 minutes, until lightly browned. Serve the ribs with fresh vegetables or salad and roasted baby potatoes.

Serves 6 to 8

Vista Verde Ranch Raspberry–White-Chocolate Cheesecake

Like many dude ranches, the Vista Verde started as a working cattle ranch. It was homesteaded in the 1920s by the Tufpley family. They began to take in a few paying guests and eventually found that "dudes" were easier to winter than cattle. The ranch has changed hands over the years and is now owned by John and Suzanne Munn, who have made it one of the best traditional guest ranches in the West.

The Vista Verde has a good riding program and offers a wide variety of other activities. In summer, guests enjoy river rafting, rock climbing, hiking, mountain biking, and nature walks. In winter, cross-country skiing and snowshoeing are favorite pastimes. After all that healthy exercise, "dudes" feel they deserve one of the chef's decadent desserts. This luscious raspberry–white-chocolate cheesecake is a ranch specialty.

1 ½ cups graham cracker crumbs

1 cup granulated sugar

6 tablespoons unsalted butter, melted

3 (8-ounce) packages cream cheese, softened

2 large eggs

2 large egg yolks

1 teaspoon almond extract

2 tablespoons unbleached all-purpose flour

½ cup mashed fresh or unsweetened frozen raspberries

6 ounces white chocolate chips, chopped

½ cup sour cream

1 ½ cups fresh raspberries

1 ½ cups fresh blueberries

Preheat the oven to 300° F.

Spray a 9^1/$_2$-by-2^1/$_2$-inch springform pan with vegetable coating spray. In a medium bowl, stir together the graham cracker crumbs and 2 tablespoons of sugar until combined. Add the butter and mix well. Press the mixture evenly onto the bottom and sides of the prepared pan.

In a large mixing bowl, using an electric mixer, beat the cream cheese until creamy. Gradually add the remaining sugar, mixing until well blended. Add the eggs and egg yolks, blending well. Add the almond extract. Stir in the flour and blend well. Scrape down the sides of the bowl and mix. Fold in the mashed raspberries and white chocolate and scrape the batter into the pan, smoothing the top with a rubber spatula. Bake for 1^1/$_4$ hours, or until firm.

Remove the cheesecake from the oven and cool at room temperature for 1 hour. Refrigerate 4 hours or overnight. Carefully run a thin-bladed knife around the outside of the cake. Open and remove the side of the pan from the cake. Carefully remove the pan bottom and transfer the cake to a serving platter. Frost the top of the cheesecake with the sour cream. Decorate with fresh raspberries and blueberries. Cut the cheesecake with a sharp knife, dipping it in hot water and wiping it dry after each slice.

Makes 12 servings

See photograph, page 188.

ACKNOWLEDGMENTS

In 1991, my husband, Gordon Black, and I moved from the Connecticut shore to Eagle Rock Ranch, located on the short grass prairie in the Chalk Bluffs just south of the Colorado-Wyoming border. Marty Jacobs and I had co-authored *Spirit of the Harvest*, and the idea for *Spirit of the West* was born when he and his wife, Linda Johnson—a talented prop stylist—visited us. The noted western historian, David Dary, and Sam Arnold—an expert on many subjects, including the cooking of mountain men and cowboys—joined our team. The book became a passion for all involved.

Eagle Rock Ranch is a very personal passion for me. My great-grandfather Benjamin Franklin Ketcham homesteaded in the Chalk Bluffs of Colorado in 1870, when this country was all open range. The Arapaho, Cheyenne, Crow, Lakota, and Pawnee all hunted and sheltered in these canyons. From the top of the bluffs, scouts spotted game and monitored the approach of friends or foes. Mountain men like Eldridge Gerry, for whom a valley and creek on the ranch are named, trapped beaver and established trading posts. Later came cowboys, rounding up free-roaming cattle, and homesteaders, making a new life on 160 acres.

This country is breathtakingly beautiful, the air is clear, the sun shines some three hundred days a year, and the sky is always dramatic, in good weather and in bad. In the 1930s and '40s my father, Mark Cox, purchased the homesteads of his Ketcham relatives. By gradually acquiring other adjoining land he put together one of the finest cattle ranches in Colorado.

I grew up on another family-owned ranch nearer to the schools and amenities of Cheyenne, but in the summer we came to Eagle Rock. I remember serving cold lemonade to cowboys thirsty after gathering cattle for branding, dipping, and vaccinating. Here the family had time to ride just for fun, and perhaps to enjoy a picnic on a bluff or by a creek. There was no telephone, and before REA put in the lines, electricity was supplied by a wind-powered generator. I'd always loved this ranch, with its colorful history and wonderful old stories of Indians, cowboys, and outlaws. As an adult coming back after many years, I was thrilled by the beauty of the land. Gordon, who is an architect, was as taken with it as I was. We sold our 1760s farmhouse on the outskirts of New Canaan, Connecticut, to try our hand at ranching.

Ranch living is not as rough as it once was. We have electricity, running water, central heating, and a satellite dish. Since we moved here, however, we've been snowed in, marooned during a flash flood, and nearly burned out by prairie fires. In spring, rain can turn the meadows into quagmires, but if the rains don't come, drought threatens the livelihood of all who live off the land. In winter, when the thermometer drops far below zero and howling winds sweep snow across these high plains, the thought of going out to hay the cattle and horses and to break the ice covering their water is not appealing, just necessary. When the sun shines again, the peace of the prairie envelops us and this is the only place we'd ever want to be. The ranchers from Mexico to Canada who contributed to this book share this passion for the land and a pride in the cowboy and ranching heritage of their families.

Our thanks go to the many wonderful people who shared their recipes and family stories with us and who gave us their support:

Chapter 1 - THE VAQUERO TRADITION IN NORTHERN MEXICO, NEW MEXICO, ARIZONA, AND CALIFORNIA: Tuda Libby Crews of Cheyenne, Wyoming, and the Libby Cattle Company, Bueyeros, New Mexico; Janell and Tio Kleberg, Julia Armstrong Partridge, Danny Martinez, Frank (Pancho) Garza, Juan Torrez, Ernesto Torres, and Johny Gonzales of the King Ranch, Kingsville, Texas; Chavela and Charlie Sellars, Bobby and Dora Spence and Gustavo Almagues of La Excondida and El Pato ranches, Coahuila, Mexico: Ivan Wilson of Benson, Arizona, and Nunn, Colorado; Florence Gillespie of Tucson, Arizona; Julie Gamez of Benson, Arizona; Angie Vindiola of St. David, Arizona; and Jean England Neubauer of the Rock Corral Ranch, Tumacacori, Arizona.

Chapter 2 - THE GREAT CATTLE DRIVES AND OPEN RANGE: Jerry and Mickey Baird of the Longtrack Ranch, Snyder, Texas; Sue Cunningham and Jean Cates, Hartley, Texas; Stella Hughes, Clifton, Arizona; Howard and LaVerne Rogers of the Brooks Ranch, Sweetwater, Texas; Carl Cooper of the Hitch Ranch, Guyman, Oklahoma; Paul Hudman of the 3 H Ranch, San Angelo, Texas; Guy, Pipp, Cathi and Doris Gillette of the Gillette Ranch, Crockett, Texas; and Sylvia and Buster Childers of the McCoy-Childers Ranch, Cheyenne, Wyoming.

Chapter 3 - THE BIG RANCHES: Helen Runnells Dubois, Washington, D.C.; John and Louise Runnells of the Runnells-Pierce Ranch, Bay City, Texas; Roger and Mary Wallace of the Little Blanco Farm, Blanco, Texas; Garland Lasater and Peggy Lasater Clark of the Lasater Ranch, Falfurrias, Texas; Dale and Janine Lasater, Lasater Ranch, Matheson, Colorado; Russell Arensman of Hong Kong; Joseph Baron Kerkerink zur Borg, Lucky Star Ranch, Chaumont, New York; Shonda Gibson, Four Sixes Ranch, Guthrie, Texas; Dr. Henry Swan III, Lakewood, Colorado; Tweet Kimball of the Cherokee Ranch, Sedalia, Colorado; the Etcheper family, Olaya Izaguirre, and La Vonna Beardsley of the Warren Livestock Company, Cheyenne, Wyoming; Kendrick Harmon of the Kendrick Cattle Company, Sheridan, Wyoming; and Cynde Georgen, Trails End Guilds, Inc., Sheridan, Wyoming.

Chapter 4 - THE HOMESTEADING ERA: Mark and Betty Cox of the Wyoming Angus Ranch, Cheyenne, Wyoming; Dorothy and Walter Ferguson, Jr., and Kimberly Ferguson of the Ferguson Ranch, Cheyenne, Wyoming; Jean Harding and Chip Harding of the Harding-Kirkbride Ranch, Meriden, Wyoming; Martha Fehlman of Powell, Wyoming; Gertrude DeMartine of Pueblo, Colorado; Janie and John Bennett of Aspen, Colorado, and the Cresent V and Garcitas ranches, Lasalle, Texas; Mrs. L.L. (Edna) Jones of Garden City, Kansas, and Ann Jones of Holcomb, Kansas; Frances Russell of Garden City, Kansas; Shelly Van Haur of the Van Haur Polled Hereford Ranch, Hilger, Montana; Jack and Joan Anderson of the Flying T Ranch, Grover, Colorado; Hattie Wilson and Pat and Jim Hubbard of Nunn, Colorado; Mark and Vicky Huls of the Huls Farm, Salem, South Dakota; John and Liz Stiefvator of Salem, South Dakota; Nancy Honig of Alexandria, South Dakota; Albert Keester of New Raymer, Colorado; Leonard and Shirley Wiggin of the Gerry Valley Ranch, Grover, Colorado; Peggy and Warren Adams of the Coal Creek Ranch, Ault, Colorado; Olive and Verle Breeden of the Box 3 Ranch, Carpenter, Wyoming; Helen Rayney Winger and Sally Peterson of the Winger Cattle Company, Johnson, Kansas; the Michelson family of the Michelson Ranch, Big Piney, Wyoming; Gretchen Noelke of the Noelke Ranch Company, Menard, Texas; Linda Vernon of Cheyenne, Wyoming; and Charlene Stogsdill of Cheyenne, Wyoming.

Chapter 5 - DUDE RANCHES: A WESTERN HERITAGE: Nancy Ferguson of the Eatons' Ranch, Wolf, Wyoming; the Van Cleve and Kirby families of the Lazy K Bar Ranch, Big Timber, Montana; the Guichon and Rose families of the Quilchena Cattle Co. and Hotel, Quilchena, British Columbia, Canada; Mary Guichon of Calgary, Alberta, Canada; Mary R. Wilson of Fort Worth, Texas; Betsy LaSelle of the Circle Z Ranch, Patagonia, Arizona; Luanne and Paul Timm of the West Pawnee Ranch Bed and Breakfast, Grover, Colorado; Skip and Chris Tilt of the Teton Ridge Ranch, Tetonia, Idaho; Clyde Nelson of The Home Ranch, Clark, Colorado; John and Suzanne Munn of the Vista Verde Ranch, Steamboat Springs, Colorado; and Bill and Pam Bryan of Off The Beaten Pack, Bozeman, Montana.

This book could never have been completed without the hard work and support of the people who assisted in typing and organization, test cooking, and prop and food styling. Many thanks to Linda DeMartine, Judy Day, Tuda Crews, Dale Black, Linda Johnson, William Smith, and Donna Sebro, each of whom put his or her heart and soul into this book.

We would like to express our appreciation for the enthusiastic support of the galleries and private collectors who lent their expertise, their cowboy artifacts, and even themselves to this project: Tim and Georgia George of Cheyenne, Wyoming, brought their beautiful chuck wagon and collection of cowboy cooking gear to Eagle Rock for location shots. Bob and James "J" Nelson and Pete Spriggs of Frontier Antiques in Cheyenne lent us many wonderful objects. "J" is also the cowboy in the photograph by the trout stream. Our neighbor Joan Anderson provided some great props, including the old cowboy lunch pail on the back cover of the book. Paula Bauman Taylor, of the Warren Heritage Museum, F. E. Warren A. F. B., Wyoming, gave us valuable advice and lent us objects from her own collection, as did the Western collectors Brenda Baker and Dr. David Ware, both of Cheyenne, Wyoming.

We would also like to thank our spouses, Gordon Black and Linda Johnson; our agent, Judith Weber; and our friends at Artisan and Workman for giving us the opportunity to write this book with the best possible support: Leslie Stoker, the publisher, let us find our way by following our own instincts and never held us back; Ann ffolliott, our editor, offered clear-headed advice and encouraged us to persevere; Jim Wageman, the designer, wove all of the visual and editorial elements into a finished book that pleased us all; Laura Lindgren cheerfully set the type; Hope Koturo saw to it that it would be produced with the very highest quality; and Beth Wareham made sure that people knew of its publication.

—BEVERLY COX AND MARTIN JACOBS

Co-author BEVERLY COX grew up on a cattle ranch near Cheyenne, Wyoming. She studied cooking in France with Mapie Toulouse-Lautrec and Gaston LeNotre and also earned a *Grande Diplome* from the Cordon Bleu in Paris. Cox is the author of ten cookbooks, including *Spirit of the Harvest: North American Indian Cooking*, winner of both James Beard and International Association of Culinary Professionals awards in 1991, which was also a collaboration with Martin Jacobs.

In 1991, after years of living in Connecticut, she and her husband, Gordon Black, moved to her family's Eagle Rock Ranch, located in the Chalk Bluffs region of Northern Colorado, and they found themselves immersed in cowboy culture. A lifelong interest in the cowboy and ranching traditions, combined with the experience of living among men and women who ride a horse as naturally as most people walk and who think nothing of roping and doctoring an ornery 600-pound steer, inspired Cox to write *Spirit of the West*.

SAM'L P. ARNOLD, who provided the book's Introduction, is a native of Denver, Colorado, and a noted western food historian, chef, restaurateur, and media personality. He is the author of *Eating up the Santa Fe Trail* and *Fryingpans West*, as well as many articles on western history. Recipes from these publications can be found on the menu of his western restaurant, The Fort, located near Morrison, Colorado, southwest of Denver.

He has been a featured speaker at the national conferences of the Western History Association and The National Wildlife Foundation, and he has lectured for the Smithsonian Institution and has received a citation from the American Association for State and Local History. Sam is also an accomplished musician, playing both the mandolin and musical saw.

His *Fryingpans West* series of television cooking shows, distributed to PBS stations across the country, has been broadcast in all 50 states, increasing America's understanding of its historic and culinary past.

DAVID DARY, who wrote the chapter introductions, is a native of Manhattan, Kansas, where his great-grandfather opened a general store in the 1860s. He lived for several years in Texas and Washington, D.C., working with CBS and NBC News, before returning to Kansas to teach journalism at the University of Kansas. He currently heads the School of Journalism at the University of Oklahoma.

Dary is the author of seven books about the West, including *Cowboy Culture*, the recipient of the Cowboy Hall of Fame Wrangler Award, the Western Writers of America's Spur Award, and the Westerners International Best Non-fiction Book Award.

MARTIN JACOBS is an award-winning photographer and author based in New York City. He has photographed many cookbooks. Jacobs and Cox collaborate regularly on a column about Indian cooking for *Native Peoples*, a magazine published by the Smithsonian's Museum of the American Indian. His love of the American West and of food history has inspired this work.

Jacobs lives in Manhattan and Bellport Village, New York, with his wife, Linda Johnson, and their Golden Retriever, Tucker.

CONVERSION CHART

Volume Equivalents

These are not exact equivalents for the American cups and spoons, but have been rounded up or down slightly to make measuring easier.

American	Metric	Imperial
$^1/_4$ t	1.25 ml	
$^1/_2$ t	2.5 ml	
1 t	5 ml	
$^1/_2$ T ($1^1/_2$ t)	7.5 ml	
1 T (3 t)	15 ml	
$^1/_4$ cup (4 T)	60 ml	2 fl. oz
$^1/_3$ cup (5 T)	75 ml	$2^1/_2$ fl oz
$^1/_2$ cup (8 T)	125 ml	4 fl oz
$^2/_3$ cup (10 T)	150 ml	5 fl oz ($^1/_4$ pint)
$^3/_4$ cup (12 T)	175 ml	6 fl oz
1 cup (16 T)	250 ml	8 fl oz
$1^1/_4$ cups	300 ml	10 fl oz
$1^1/_2$ cups	350 ml	12 fl oz
1 pint (2 cups)	500 ml	16 fl oz
1 quart (4 cups)	1 litre	$1^3/_4$ pints

Weight Equivalents

The metric weights given in this chart are not exact equivalents, but have been rounded up or down slightly to make measuring easier.

Oven Temperature Equivalents

Avoirdupois	Metric	Avoirdupois	Metric
$^1/_4$ oz	7 g	12 oz	350 g
$^1/_2$ oz	15 g	13 oz	375 g
1 oz	30 g	14 oz	400 g
2 oz	60 g	15 oz	425 g
3 oz	90 g	16 oz (1 lb)	450 g
4 oz	115 g	1 lb 2 oz	00 g
5 oz	150 g	$1^1/_2$ lb	750 g
6 oz	175 g	2 lb	900 g
7 oz	200 g	$2^1/_4$ lb	1 kg
8 oz ($^1/_2$ lb)	225 g	3 lb	1.4 kg
9 oz	250 g	4 lb	1.8 kg
10 oz	300 g	$4^1/_2$ lb	2 kg
11 oz	325 g		

Oven	°F.	°C.	Gas Mark
very cool	250–275	130–140	$^1/_2$–1
cool		300	150 2
warm		325	170 3
moderate	350	180	4
moderately hot	375	190	5
	400	200	6
hot	425	220	7
very hot	450	230	8
	475	250	9

APPENDIX

Chilies

When handling hot chilies, wear rubber gloves and keep your hands away from eyes and other sensitive areas. Capsaicin, the source of the heat, is concentrated in the ribs and seeds. If you want to cut down on the heat, remove them.

To peel chilies, make a small slit near the stem end. Preheat the oven to 400°F. Spread on a baking sheet and roast, turning often, until all sides are black and blistered. You may also roast chilies directly over a gas flame or on a grill over hot coals. Spread a damp towel over roasted chilies and allow to cool. Carefully pull and scrape skin from cooled chilies.

Chorizo

A highly seasoned pork sausage used in Spain and Mexican cooking. Mexican chorizo is made with fresh pork, while the Spanish version is made from smoked pork. To use Mexican chorizo, remove the casing, crumble, and sauté.

Corn or Maize Products

Atole Finely ground, toasted blue cornmeal. It is boiled with water or milk and served as a porridge or a hot drink.

Chicos Whole corn kernels that are first steamed, then dried and stored for future use. Chicos are reconstituted by soaking in water and boiling until tender.

Field Corn Flint or field corn (*Zea indurata*) is used as fodder for animals and is ground into corn meal, used in making polenta and cornbread. Field corn has more starch than sweet corn. When substituting pureed sweet corn in a recipe calling for field corn, it may be necessary to add 1 to 2 tablespoons of masa harina to make a firmer mixture.

Hominy An Anglicized Algonquin term for corn kernels that have been soaked or boiled with hardwood ashes, unslaked lime, or caustic soda to remove their tough outer hulls, a process that also increases the available nutrients. Dried hominy may be rinsed well and cooked or ground directly after this process or dried again to be stored until needed.

Masa Meal made from grinding wet hominy. Used to make tortillas and tamales. Masa that has been dried is called *Masa Harina*.

Lard

This semisolid rendered pork fat is excellent for pastry making and deep fat frying and ranks with butter in digestibility. Lard is actually lower in saturated fat than butter; $3^1/_2$ ounces of lard contains 39.2 grams of saturated fat, while $3^1/_2$ ounces of butter contains 50.5 grams of saturated fat.

Lime

Pickling lime, sold in the canning section of grocery stores, is used to crisp cucumber slices in some old-fashioned pickle recipes. Although hydrated lime from garden and hardware stores is sometimes substituted, the USDA does not recommend its use. In any case, precautions need to be taken when using lime. Do not breathe the fumes from the powder and rinse the cucumber slices very thoroughly in several changes of fresh cold water after soaking in the lime solution to remove any residue.

COOKBOOKS

Chuckwagon Recipes and Others
Sue Cunningham and Jean Cates
P.O. Box 22, 9th and Smith,
Hartley, Texas. [Zip tk]
Tel: (806) 365-4596

King Ranch Cookbook
(Proceeds benefit the Santa Gertrudis and Laureles
schools)
King Ranch Saddle Shop, Inc.
201 East Kleberg
P.O. Box 1594
Kingsville, Texas 78363
Tel: (512) 595-5761
(800) 282-KING

Martha's Pioneer Cookbook, Wyoming Centennial Edition
Martha Fehlman
640 Avenue F.
Powell, Wyoming 82435

BEANS, CHILES, PILONCILLO, AND CORN PRODUCTS

Santa Cruz Chili and Spice Company
P.O. Box 177
Tumacacori, Arizona 85640
Tel: (520) 398-2591

Wyoming Championship Chugwater Chili
Chugwater Chili Corporation
P.O. Box 92
Chugwater, WY 82210
Tel: (307) 422-3345

Los Chileros de Nuevo Mexico
P.O. Box 6215
Santa Fe, New Mexico 87502
Tel: (505) 471-6967

Jerry's All-Purpose Seasoning
Winner of the World Championship Cabrito Cookoff
Jerry Baird
2363 Uvalde
Snyder, Texas 79549
Tel: (915) 573-8389

CHOKECHERRY JAM

The Baer Family
4130 County Road 207
Carpenter, Wyoming 82054

GAME

The Game Exchange
107 Quint Street
San Francisco, California 91424
Tel: (415) 282-7878 or (800) 426-3872

La Maison de Chevreuil
421 St. Paul East, Suite 200
Montreal, Quebec
Canada H2Y 1H5
Tel: (514) 282-1996

DUTCH OVENS AND OTHER CAMPFIRE COOKING EQUIPMENT

Lehman's Non-Electric Catalog
One Lehman Circle, P.O. Box 41
Kidron, Ohio 44636
Tel: (216) 857-5757
Fax: (216) 857-5785

TRAVEL

Off The Beaten Path: Personal Itinerary Planning for
the Rocky Mountain West
Bill and Pam Bryan
109 East Main Street
Bozeman, Montana 59715
Tel: (406) 586-1311
Fax: (406) 787-4147

FEATURED DUDE RANCHES

Eatons' Ranch
Wolf, Wyoming 82844
Tel: (307) 655-9285
Season: June 1–October 1
Ranch activities and amenities:
Horseback riding, fly-fishing, swimming pool
Guest Capacity: 125
Airport: Sheridan, Wyoming

Lazy K Bar Ranch
P. O. Box 550
Big Timber, Montana 59011
Tel: (406) 537-4404

Season: June 23–Labor Day
Ranch activities and amenities:
Horseback riding (including overnight rides),
working cattle, hiking, fly-fishing, fossil-hunting,
swimming pool
Guest Capacity: 35–40
Airports: Billings or Bozeman, Montana

Quilchena Cattle Company and Hotel
Box 1
Quilchena, B.C.
Canada VOE 2RO
Tel: (604) 378-2611
Fax: (604) 378-6091
Season: April 25–October 15
Ranch activities and amenities:
Horseback riding, swimming, wind-surfing, fishing,
mountain biking, hiking, golf and tennis, restaurant,
coffee shop, and saloon
Guest capacity: 38
Airport: private airstrip for small planes, Vancouver;
Kamloops, B.C., for commercial flights

Circle Z Ranch
Patagonia, Arizona 85624
Tel: (520) 393-2525
Season: November 1–May 15
Ranch activities and amenities:
Horseback riding, overnight pack trips, bird-
watching, tennis, heated swimming pool
Off Ranch: Golf and fishing
Airports: Tucson or Nogales (for private planes), Arizona

West Pawnee Ranch Bed and Breakfast
WCR 130
Grover, Colorado 80729
Tel: (970) 895-2482
Season: year round
Ranch activities and amenities:
Horseback riding, roping lessons, buggy rides,
bird-watching
Guest capacity: 4–6
Airport: Denver International Airport, Colorado

Teton Ridge Ranch
200 Valley View Road
Tetonia, Idaho 83452
Seasons: Summer: May 15–November 1; Winter:
December 15–April 1
Ranch activities and amenities:
Horseback riding, fly-fishing, sporting clays,

overnight pack trips, cross-country skiing,
snowmobiling, dog-sledding
Guest capacity: 10–12
Airports: Idaho Falls, Idaho, or Jackson, Wyoming

The Home Ranch
P.O. Box 822
Clark, CO 80428
Tel: (970) 879-1780
Fax (970) 879-1795
Seasons: Summer: June 2–October 6; Winter: Mid-
December–April 1
Ranch activities and amenities:
Horseback riding, fly-fishing, hiking, heated swimming
pool, hot tub and sauna, cabins with private hot tubs
Guest Capacity: 50
Airports: Yampa Valley Regional Airport, Hayden,
Colorado (shuttle to ranch), or Denver International
Airport.

Skyline Guest Ranch
P. O. Box 67
Telluride, CO 81435
Tel: (970) 728-3757
Fax: (970) 728-6728
Seasons: Summer: June 1–September; Winter:
December 15–April 1
Ranch activities and amenities:
Horseback riding, fly-fishing, mountain biking,
hiking, alpine and cross-country skiing, boot hockey,
sledding, snow-shoeing
Guest capacity: 35
Airport: Telluride, Colorado

Vista Verde Ranch
P. O. Box 465
Steamboat Springs, CO 80477
Tel: (970) 879-3858
(800) 526-7433
Fax: (970) 897-1413
Seasons: Summer: Last week of May–end of
September; Winter: December 15–Mid-March
Ranch activities and amenities: Horseback riding,
cross-country skiing
Guest capacity: 25–30
Airport: Tampa Valley Regional Airport, Hayden,
Colorado, or Denver International Airport

Arnold, Sam. *FryingPans West*. Sam Arnold, 1985.

Arnold, Sam'l P. *Eating Up The Santa Fe Trail*. Niwot, CO: 1990.

Blakeslee, E.C., Emma Leslie and H. Hughes. *The Compendium of Cookery and Reliable Recipes*. Chicago: The Merchants' Specialty Co., 1890.

Braun, Matt. *Matt Braun's Western Cooking*. Chicago: Contemporary Books, 1988.

Bryant, Tom and Joel Bernstein. *A Taste of Ranching: Cooks and Cowboys*. Albuquerque, NM: Border Books, 1993.

Carlton, Jan McBride. *The Old-Fashion Cookbook*. New York: Weathervane Books, 1979.

Clark, Morton G. *The Wide, Wide World of Texas*. New York: Bonanza Books, n.d.

Clayton, Lawrence and J.U. Salvant. *Historic Ranches of Texas*. Austin: University of Texas Press, 1993.

Cooking in Wyoming: Women's Suffrage Centennial Edition. Casper, WY: Bighorn Book Company, 1965.

Cunningham, Sue and Jean Cates. *Chuck Wagon Recipes and Others*. Lenaxa, KS. Cookbook Publishers, Inc., 1994.

Dary, David. *Cowboy Culture: Saga of Five Centuries*. Lawrence, KS: University Press of Kansas, 1989.

DeLeon, Arnoldo. *The Tejano Community, 1836–1900*. Albuquerque, NM: University of New Mexico Press, 1982.

Durham, Philip and Everette Jones. *The Negro Cowboys*. Lincoln, NE: University of Nebraska Press, 1965.

Favorite Recipes. Lincoln, NE: The Ladies Aid of Our Savior's Lutheran Church.

Flood, Elizabeth Clair. *Old-Time Dude Ranches Out West*. Salt Lake City: Gibbs Smith Publishers, 1995.

Fehlman, Martha. *Martha's Pioneer Cookbook, Wyoming Centennial Edition*. Powell, Wyoming,

Georgen, Cynde. *One Cowboy's Dream, John B. Kendrick: His Family, Home, and Ranching Empire*. Sheridan, WY: Trail End Guilds, Inc., 1995.

Green, Donald E. *Panhandler Pioneer: Henry Hitch, this Ranch, and this Family*. Norman: Oklahoma Heritage Association, Inc., University of Oklahoma Press, 1978.

Luchetti, Cathy. *Home on the Range: A Culinary History of the American West*. New York: Villard Books, 1993.

Hughes, Stella. *Chuck Wagon Cooking*. Tucson, AZ: The University of Arizona Press, 1974.

Kerby, Bob. *Range Riders Cookin'*. Kearney, NE: Bob Kerby Longhorn Studio, 1989.

King Ranch Cook Book. Kingsville, TX: King Ranch Inc., 1992.

Koenig, Ernestine. *Pawnee County*. Greeley, CO: The Pawnee Historical Society, 1979.

Jordan, Teresa. *Cowgirls: Women of the American West*. Lincoln: University of Nebraska Press, 1982.

Laramie County Cow-Bells. *Beef and More*. Waverly, LA: G & R Publishing, Co., Press of K.C., 1961.

Kirkbride, Mrs. Dan. *From These Roots*. Meridan, WY: Mrs. Dan Kirkbride, 1972.

Kreidberg, Marjorie. *Food on the Frontier: Minnesota Cooking*. St. Paul: Minnesota Historical Society Press, 1975.

McDowell, Bart. *The American Cowboy in Life and Legend*. Washington D.C.: National Geographic Society, 1972.

Medley, Wild Wes. *Original Cowboy Cookbook*. Hurricane, WY: Wes Medley-Original Western Publications, 1989.

Omtvedt, Tamara and Krister Bespalic, eds. *The Oregon Trail Cookbook*. Kearney, NE: Morris Publishing, 1993.

Owens, Frances E. *Mrs. Owens' Cook Book and Useful Household Hints*. Little Rock, AR: J.M. Ball, 1888.

Peyton, James W. *La Cocina de la Frontera: Mexican-American Cooking from the Southwest*. Santa Fe, NM: Red Crane Books, 1994.

Preston, Mark. *California Mission Cookery*. Albuquerque, NM: 1994.

Price, B. Byron. *National Cowboy Hall of Fame Chuck Wagon Cookbook*. New York: Hearst Books, 1995.

Stratton, Joanna L. *Pioneer Women: Voices from the Kansas Frontier*. New York: Simon & Schuster, 1981.

Trail Boss's Cowboy Cookbook. Society for Range Management, 1985.

Van Cleve, Barbara. *Hard Twist, Western Ranch Women*. Santa Fe, N.M.: Museum of New Mexico Press, 1995.

White, Richard. *"It's Your Misfortune and None My Own": A New History of the American West*. Norman: University of Oklahoma Press, 1991.

Williams, Jacqueline. *Wagon Wheel Kitchens: Food on the Oregon Trail*. Lawrence, KA: University of Kansas Press, 1993.

Williams, Mary L., ed. *An Army Wife's Cookbook*. Tucson, AZ: Southwest Parks and Monuments Association, 1972.

Williamson, Darcy. *Basque Cooking and Lore*. Caldwell, ID: Caxton Publishers Inc., 1993.

I N D E X

DESIGNED BY JIM WAGEMAN

TYPEFACES IN THIS BOOK ARE
BASSUTO, DESIGNED BY PAUL HICKSON,
CELESTIA ANTIQUA, DESIGNED BY MARK VAN BRONKHORST,
AND PRISTINA, DESIGNED BY PHILL GRIMSHAW

THE TYPE WAS SET AND LAYOUTS WERE CREATED
BY LAURA LINDGREN, NEW YORK

PRINTED AND BOUND BY
ARTEGRAFICA S.P.A.
VERONA, ITALY